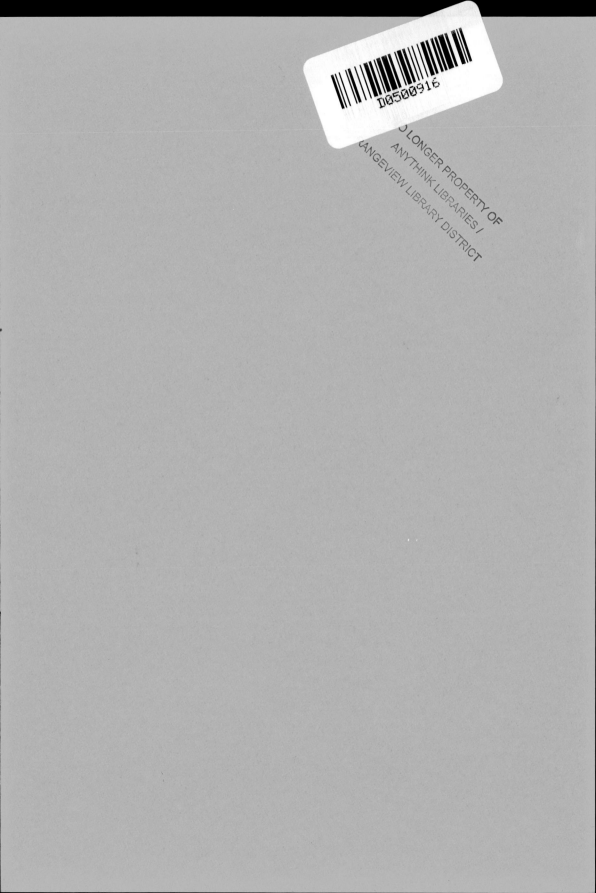

Find Your Pleasure

THE ART OF LIVING A MORE JOYFUL LIFE

CYNTHIA LOYST

Published by Simon & Schuster

New York   London   Toronto   Sydney   New Delhi

SIMON &
SCHUSTER
CANADA

Simon & Schuster Canada
A Division of Simon & Schuster, Inc.
166 King Street East, Suite 300
Toronto, Ontario M5A 1J3

Portions of this book have been published previously on findyourpleasure.com.
See page 267 for photo credits.

This Simon & Schuster Canada edition January 2020

SIMON & SCHUSTER CANADA and colophon are trademarks of Simon & Schuster, Inc.

For information about special discounts for bulk purchases,
please contact Simon & Schuster Special Sales at
1-800-268-3216 or CustomerService@simonandschuster.ca.

Interior design by Jessica L. Boudreau

Manufactured in the United States of America

10 9 8 7 6 5 4 3 2 1

Library and Archives Canada Cataloguing in Publication
Title: Find your pleasure / by Cynthia Loyst.
Names: Loyst, Cynthia, 1974– author.
Identifiers: Canadiana (print) 20190096276 | Canadiana (ebook) 20190096284 |
    ISBN 9781508259336 (hardcover) | ISBN 9781508259343 (ebook)
Subjects: LCSH: Women—Psychology. | LCSH: Pleasure. | LCSH: Self-realization.
Classification: LCC HQ1206 .L68 2020 | DDC 155.3/339—dc23

ISBN 978-1-5082-5933-6
ISBN 978-1-5082-5934-3 (ebook)

For Jason and Jaya,
my favorite pleasures

CONTENTS

A NOTE FROM CYNTHIA

Picture this.

It was 2013, a Friday in November. I was frantically typing at my tragically disorganized desk upstairs from a TV studio. Attached to me was a strange contraption rhythmically drawing every last drop of milk from my inflated boobs—something I did several times a day while at work.

I had been recently hired as one of five hosts on a brand-new daily live talk show called *The Social*. Although there was a lot of pressure on this new TV show, I tried to reassure myself that I was chosen for a reason, that there was lots to be happy about: I was a new mom with an amazing job, a supportive partner, solid friendships, and a healthy, thriving child.

However, there was a near-constant din in my head sinking me into an abyss of self-doubt, must-dos, should-dos, and never-ending to-do lists. I wondered: *Is my son getting enough milk? Is he sleeping right? Am I a good partner? Do I suck at my job? Should I lose weight? Do I need Botox to look good? Did I send those bloody thank-you cards? Who's making dinner tonight?!*

As I rushed to disentangle myself from my mammary machine to go to set, I knocked over one of my hard-won bottles of milk. I fought back tears, fumbled through rehearsal and hair and makeup touch-ups. As the show went live, I felt like I was dying. But I stayed upright, and when my colleagues asked afterward if I was okay, I enthusiastically said, "Of course!"

I was not okay. In fact I cried all the way home. I knew I wasn't depressed, exactly. I just felt like I had lost a part of me. Or several parts. Even though I was eating every day, I hadn't been savoring anything. Despite the fact that I was working at an exciting job with wonderful people, I was in no way delighted. And while I was trying to do everything, I wasn't living deeply. I had lost connection to all the things that once brought me pleasure.

I reached out to my closest girlfriends and asked, "When was the last time you did or felt something immensely pleasurable?" Their answers ranged from "Years ago" to "No idea" to "Haaahaaaaaa."

It became clear to me that something was missing in our lives. It was as if we'd all been given the message that pleasure was the dirty cousin to happiness, that the things we desired were the exact things we shouldn't be reaching for. The women I knew (especially those of us who grew up in conservative or religious households) were receiving this message the worst. We were convinced that if we indulged too much—in the boardroom, bakery, or bedroom—we would become bossy, fat, or slutty, all of which were supposedly unlovable characteristics. This anti-pleasure messaging was designed, it seemed to me, to keep women silenced, shamed, and deprived. That's when I decided that encouraging women to boldly claim and prioritize pleasures was a deeply feminist act.

I began a deep dive into pleasure.

I took long, hot baths while sipping cool, citrusy glasses of white wine.

I ignored piles of laundry to play with my son, Jaya.

I planted savory herbs and bought flowers for myself.

I baked complicated cupcakes and ate them without guilt.

I wrapped myself in cozy blankets and took unapologetic naps.

I slowed down.

I moved my body. I touched it, too.

I rediscovered my passion for writing, which resulted in the creation of an online destination, findyourpleasure.com.

As I began seeking out the many pleasures in my life, I realized I was becoming happier, healthier, and more confident. Every time I lost focus and fell into the service of must-dos and should-dos, I slipped back into a pleasure deficit—becoming anxious, brittle, and anti-sensual.

The experience was a revelation.

• • •

This book is a collection of the ways in which I rediscovered pleasure in the most unexpected and even obvious spaces. I wrote it for all of us who have at some point lost a true connection to our deepest pleasures, as a reminder of all the things that are delicious and delightful if we're awake enough to acknowledge them.

It's my hope, dear reader, that you will see yourself in these stories and that they will be not only a pleasure to read but will also inspire you to uncover new (or long-forgotten) pleasures. Along with sharing stories about my friends and my son, Jaya, I also write about Jason, my common-law partner of almost twenty years. I refer to him as "partner" because we're a team and that term brings us both pleasure. But when you're reading, use whatever term feels comfy to you. Same thing goes with gender, identity, and so on.

I also swear a bit in here. It's not my intention to shock or offend, but the occasional, well-timed expletive for descriptive purposes is intensely pleasurable for me. If that's not the case for you, feel free to mentally replace those words with whatever tickles your fancy. And on that note, I hope that whether you start from the front of the book and read cover to cover or choose random pages to enjoy, all of your fancies are tickled. I've heard many artists describe their work as already existing—that it's simply a matter of peeling back layers to find what lies beneath. Similarly, you are already primed for pleasure. All you have to do is reach down and discover it inside.

Now, consider me your official pleasure pusher!

THE KEYS TO PLEASURE

I'm often asked, "How can I get more pleasure out of my life right now?" Here's my answer.

Just say, "AAAH." While there's no doubt that taking in a deep breath and sighing out "Aaah" will automatically make you feel better, AAAH is actually an acronym to remind you of the four keys to pleasure: awareness + attention + authenticity + help = pleasure.

This simple formula can help you start building a life of pleasure today.

Awareness

What gives someone else deep pleasure may not do a thing for you, so become aware of what you truly love. Are there things you used to do that have fallen to the wayside? Is there something you've always wanted to try? If you had a free day to yourself, what would you choose to do? If money weren't an issue, what work would you do? These questions are just a start, but they'll get you thinking about where your passion lies. And where there's passion, there's pleasure.

Attention

Life can get busy, and sometimes we forget to pay attention to moments of joy, but part of experiencing a life of pleasure is being mindful of the incredible delights your senses have to offer. You can also find pleasure by directing your attention away from the present moment and mindfully tuning into your fantasies, which helps you envision new realities, stokes your imagination, or just provides a much-needed mental escape. The key to both mindfulness and escapism is the power of the mind.

Authenticity

Sometimes it's hard to find pleasure because we're not living in a way that is truthful for us. Sometimes we are in denial about what we actually want for our lives or how we are getting in our own way and maybe even contributing to our own problems. Maybe you're struggling with a physical or emotional issue, or maybe something or someone in your life is a problem masquerading as a plea-sure. This is where authenticity and honesty come in. Ask yourself: *Who am I? What am I seeking and why? Is this a pleasure I control, or does it control me?* It's not always easy to answer these questions, but when you do, you'll find that acknowledging and embracing what you truly find pleasurable is liberating.

Help

Everyone struggles at some point under the weight of to-do lists at home and at work. If you find yourself in this situation, ask for help, even if it's for something small. Carving out time for yourself—even five minutes—is important because it sets the stage for pleasure to happen, and the more you create these moments, the more pleasure you will receive.

The next time you start to wonder how to bring more pleasure into your life, re-member these four keys and you'll be well on your way.

Friends
&
Family

SAVORING MOMENTS

Recently I was with friends watching our kids play together and we lamented how quickly time passes.

Then one of them shared a meditative perspective on impermanence. As the story goes, there was once a master holding a glass who said, "Someone gave me this glass; I really like it. It holds my water and glistens in the sunlight. When I tap it, it makes a lovely sound. One day the wind may blow it off the shelf or my elbow may knock it off the table and it will shatter. When I understand that the glass is already broken, every moment with it is precious."

In other words, life is unpredictable and always changing. So whether it is food, drink, sex, or silliness—savor it all.

Indulge Yourself

Cuddle something soft and squishy. Cashmere, puppies, and babies all count.

FIND YOUR PLEASURE

SOUL MATES

My friend and musician Jann Arden once told me she believes that packs of souls travel together. I love this image because we've all had that feeling, haven't we? You know, when you meet someone and almost immediately feel as if you've known them your entire life?

When I was six years old, a sunny new girl, appropriately named Sunday, showed up at our school and we became instant friends. Through the years, we played together, danced together, laughed together, and shared all our hopes and fears. We sadly lost touch in our late teens, but one day, we ran into each other on the street and picked right up where we left off. Now and then, we message each other about something we said or did decades ago, and our private joke will still send us into instant stitches.

That is the power and pleasure of good friends.

Pleasure Prompt

Solve a puzzle, grab some Play-Doh, or unearth another childhood game you've forgotten about.

FIND YOUR PLEASURE

AL FRESCO FUN

What is it about dining al fresco that is so seductive? When winter thaws into spring, there's that primal pull to break bread with others outdoors like our ancestors must have done. Do you feel it? I do. And in our ever busy and often isolated worlds, picnics with friends remind us of the simple pleasures of connecting through sharing food.

The very sight of a picnic basket conjures up childhood memories of adventures. And whether it's so-called guilty pleasure foods—burgers, hot dogs, chips— or sophisticated ones—pungent cheeses, crusty bread, fresh fruits, crisp veggies, a carafe of wine—deciding what you'll take along to enjoy is half the fun.

But picnics are often best when they're spontaneous and fairly effortless. When you try too hard to plan "the perfect picnic," that's invariably when napkins begin to fly around, ants congregate, or the person beside you in the park or at the beach starts smoking. Instead, focus on the friends and family you're with. If you have them (and a stocked picnic basket), you have a recipe for pure pleasure.

Indulge Yourself

Eat something mini: a mini cupcake, mini pickle, mini dumpling.

FIND YOUR PLEASURE

THE JOY OF EATING

Picture yourself savoring lemon cake drizzled with lavender-infused honey. Imagine licking your fingers after delighting in dark chocolate truffles filled with salted caramel ganache. Now think of sipping a buttery white wine paired with creamy cheeses served on crispy bread. Hungry yet?

I first noticed how intuitive our connection to food when watching my newborn son shimmy his way up my breasts to plant his mouth on one of them. As I watched him suckle his way from crying to calm, it dawned on me that this is likely the time when many of us develop our long-standing love affair with food.

Yet that connection can be fraught. How many of us describe food as "good" or "bad"? Felt guilt after eating certain things? Been warned of the perils of indulgence? In these ways, we may feel disconnected from this essential joy, but eating is a cornucopia of overlapping pleasures and benefits.

Those who savor meals and eat slowly are likely to eat less and digest more efficiently. The more attractive the food, the better it is for us—one study showed that people absorbed certain minerals in food better when they consumed a beautiful-looking meal. If you've had a cold, you know that eating without the sense of smell can turn food into an array of not-entirely-satisfying textures. Yet when all our senses work together, the tactile nature of foods—crunchy, melty, sticky, gooey, unctuous—can take our experience from basic to fantastic.

There is also a huge connection between food and sex. Anyone who has ever looked at the fleshy insides of a ripe fig or fondled a turgid zucchini has probably contemplated their uncanny resemblance to the body's pleasure zones. There's even an entire sexual fetish called "splosh" dedicated to the delights of combining foods like whipped cream with the naked body. As Bunny Crumpacker notes in her delicious book *The Sex Life of Food*, a good cook is a lot like a good lover—possessing an understanding of pacing, timing, and how to combine elements that will lead to an explosion of pleasure.

So eat what pleases you—just make sure you deeply enjoy every moment of it.

GAME NIGHTS

Games were big in my house when I was growing up. At my parents' dinner parties, we kids would often play under the dining room table while a fierce round of cards was taking place up above. A rite of passage occurred when we were invited to play a game with the adults. We knew we had to pay attention, be strategic, and stay awake until the bitter end, lest we not be invited again.

Now that I'm the adult with a child of my own, I can see the incredible importance of game nights. They're an opportunity to turn screens off and make time for face-to-face family bonding, and the fact that you have to follow rules, take turns, and be a good loser teaches the skills needed to be a good human.

There's a game out there for everyone now: people who love numbers, words, or storytelling, those who love art or sports, and history buffs or thrill seekers. Or expand your sense of adventure by checking out a board game café or visiting an escape room.

The fun of doing something new and challenging not only helps expand your mind but keeps you feeling connected, too. I'm still discovering new things about my partner, Jason, via games, even after almost twenty years together, and that sense of play has brought unexpected pleasures into our relationship.

FIND YOUR PLEASURE

LOVE LETTERS

Growing up, my mother was the main lunch-maker in our household. Most of her lunches were forgettable—a little bologna here, a wiener in a hot-water thermos there. But one day she did something different. As I sat down with my friends for lunch, I was delighted to discover that nestled in between the juice box and the cookies there was a little folded love note.

I don't remember exactly what it said—something simple like, "I love you. Have a great day!" And I don't know what inspired this tiny gesture, but the impact was huge.

Since then, I have written and received many love letters. I have a box filled with handwritten notes: some from young men filled with angst and desire, others from wonderful friends I don't get to see enough, and, of course, ones from my son written in jagged letters. Looking through them is a visual and tactile experience that conjures up pleasure-soaked memories.

There's nothing wrong with a letter written in electronic form. There's also the added bonus of being able to add in a saucy/silly emoji or a voice note for your loves to listen to. But there is something extra special about handwriting something to someone you care about.

So pick up a pen today and tell someone you love them. It doesn't take much to take someone's day from mundane to magical.

DRAWER FULL OF MEMORIES

Raise your hand if you have "that" drawer. You know, the one filled with memories.

There's a drawer in my son's room that has the little white knitted hat he wore home from the hospital, a collection of swaddling blankets, and a sweater with a dinosaur knitted by my maternal grandmother.

Every once in a while, I take these items out and look at them, smell them, and reflect on how much this little person has changed. These objects instantly bring me back to a time when his mouth was all gums and constantly sweet breath. When he first started learning to talk and the sound of his little voice and the silly things he used to say. The deep pleasure of these moments reminds me of the potent energy of objects.

Your memory drawer might have a lock of hair, a first-place ribbon, or a pair of booties. These objects allow us to conjure—even just for a moment—the past, and are transformed from a collection of "things" into little time machines, reminding us that no matter how much our children grow and change, they will always be our babies.

Mine holds a collection of random things, including a pair of well-loved shark booties from the early steps my son took, a bejeweled bra I wore during my belly-dancing days, a hand-woven choker that my grandmother brought back from Africa, and stones collected from my travels around the world.

Pleasure Project

Take some of your children's favorite artworks and reimagine them.
You can make them into clothing or jewelry or even cuddly stuffed creations.

FIND YOUR PLEASURE

QUALITY TIME

We all have a friend we see only once or twice a year, but when we do, we somehow manage to pick up right where we left off. That kind of connection comes from years of shared history, and meaningful exchanges—conversations that aren't about platitudes or gossip, but genuine emotion and vulnerability.

Whether you're marking an important milestone or simply making time for a quick meet-up, make your get-togethers with special people in your life experiences you'll never forget. The effects can last a lifetime.

My co-hosts on *The Social* and I have rented a hotel room several times for an overnight stay and stayed up until the wee hours of the morning and, honestly, between the consumption of junk food, playing of silly board games, and questionable booze choices, it feels like we're back in high school. It not only brings us closer together, but we also escape our day-to-day routines in ways that are truly unforgettable.

But you don't have to pull an all-nighter in order to have a memorable time. Why not go see a beloved musician from your youth? Or how about checking out that new coffee shop that's moved into the space where you whiled away time together when you were young?

There are so many ways to dig into the alchemy of your friendships and mine golden moments.

Indulge Yourself

Take the long way home. Maybe even get a little lost.

THE LANGUAGE OF FOOD

There weren't a lot of rules in our house growing up, but one of them was that we all sat at the table and ate dinner together. It was a time for us to connect, share stories of our day, and discuss exciting things that we were looking forward to.

I remember going to a friend's house for dinner and being absolutely shocked to discover that they ate completely in silence. But that was their ritual—I'm sure they would have found the loud chaos of my family's dinners equally disconcerting.

The ritual of family meals is not just for pleasure—it also has a purpose. Research has shown that adolescents who regularly eat meals with their families are less depressed, less likely to have used drugs, and have higher grade-point averages.

Something important takes place when we eat together: people young and old open up and share their emotions as they share food. No matter our age or culture, the one love language we all speak is the language of food. If you add in other elements to delight the senses—like lighting a candle or putting on music—you enhance the ritual even more.

FIND YOUR PLEASURE

HOLIDAYS

T ell me something I can look forward to."

When I was a little girl, I would always ask this while being tucked into bed. My mother would invariably tell me wonderful things about upcoming holidays in what I imagine were the hopes that I would float off to sleep with visions of sugary treats dancing around in my small head.

Halloween was a special joy. The thrill of getting dressed up in elaborate costumes with friends and going to visit people in our neighborhood in exchange for candy is truly a childhood definition of pleasure. I also loved Easter for the magic of the egg hunt, and I swooned for the romance of Valentine's Day.

But my favorite holiday was and still is Christmas. Even as a now-unsecular woman, I can look back and see how the religious core of this holiday infused it with some of its most memorable aspects: the nativity scene, midnight mass, and angel decorations.

Speaking of angels, my mother had a little chime set. When the candles were lit, tiny angels on it twirled, seemingly by magic. I would stare at them while listening to Christmas carols and make secret wishes. Each year, pulling a box from our basement with the words *XMAS Decorations* on it, unpacking the tissue paper, and unearthing these golden cherubs, I felt such glee. Now, when my son and I take out our ornaments, I see the same spark in his eyes that mine must have had, as he recalls those tiny pleasures he's forgotten over the past year.

No matter what holidays your family celebrates, I'll bet the pleasures are the same—the sounds of your family connecting over age-old traditions, the smells of nostalgia-infused home-cooked meals, perhaps even the delight of curling up in your childhood bed.

Now that it's me tucking my son into bed, I've come to understand just what my mother wished the future held for me, and it's the same things I wish for my son: health and happiness and that some of his fondest memories will include the pleasures of celebrating important days with family.

Indulge Yourself

Watch your children sleeping.

FIND YOUR PLEASURE

PEOPLE PLEASING

I remember that in the fog of post-birth, exhausted, all I could think was "Must . . . get . . . thank-you . . . cards . . . out." It was so important that I not disappoint my mother and friends that I was willing to forgo much-needed sleep to get the cards written.

This sort of thing is something we call emotional labor: those small, niggling duties that make domestic life run smoothly. It's been shown that women spend more than double the time on them than men do. (Insert sigh.) Why? Women are raised to be people pleasers.

Once, I received an email from a mother at my son's preschool about gifts for teachers. She undoubtedly had the loveliest of intentions, but I panicked. How much money should I give? Should I get gifts for all the teachers? When would I have the time?! I called my partner, and he said, "Don't worry. You don't have to do anything."

Easy for him to say. He doesn't have to wear the dreaded shame of being a woman who doesn't live up to certain expectations. Seriously, does a man ever get the side-eye from anyone for forgetting a birthday gift? Or for not sending a thank-you card?

I know there are women who don't view emotional labor as taxing. I see them on Instagram and marvel at their hand-created name tags lovingly sewn into their kids' clothes, and their gorgeous homemade confections specially made for school bake sales. But not every woman is capable of or interested in these types of things.

So when you say to your guests, "Bring nothing but yourselves," mean it. When someone forgets a thank-you card, remember when you were caught up in the chaos of life and give them a pass. Think about why a woman might not be able to meet your expectations and ask yourself, "Does it really matter?" or "Why don't I expect this from men?" Imagine what we could accomplish—and how we'd feel—if we didn't care as much about all this stuff. If that weight was lifted off us. So how about we start by lifting that weight off one another?

FIND YOUR PLEASURE

THE HEALING POWER OF
LAUGHTER

Isn't laughter one of the most pleasurable experiences in life? Someone says or does something wacky, or you recall a particular funny memory, and you feel the eruption begin. It may start with a smile, evolve into a chuckle, and then those rhythmic contractions unfold from deep within your belly. Before you know it, rivers of tears are streaming down your face and you can do nothing but give yourself over to the sheer joy of it all.

Laughter has healing properties, too. My doula told me to find a comedian who I found funny and to watch videos of him or her performing when I was in early labor with my son. She believes that when we laugh, the deepest parts of ourselves begin to relax and that helps us manage pain. While I won't say my labor was pain-free, it was definitely much more manageable than I ever would have imagined—and, in some parts, even pleasurable.

So how about that? Laughter as a prescription for pleasure. Perhaps it can truly heal the most painful parts of life.

Indulge Yourself

Recall a memory that makes you laugh till you cry, or cry until you laugh.

SNORT GLITTER

I once overheard a criminal defense lawyer—someone quite serious—declare that if she could, she would dip her face in glitter and snort it just before entering a courtroom. In that moment I fell in love with her.

One of my friends once said that she loved a truffle mushroom soup so much she wanted to inject it into her vagina. I laughed until tears slipped down my cheeks—not only because that was a hilarious thing to say but also because I immediately understood the type of pleasure she was describing.

Inspired by these two women, I suggest we imagine all the ways we can snort, inject, devour, and fuck small pleasures into our lives, and then share them with others. But only those pleasures that could never harm us or the people we love. Pleasures that will inspire, conjure love, or give rise to laughter (or all of those).

FIND YOUR PLEASURE

LETTING GO

L ife is a constant exercise in letting go. We all grow up with expectations of who we'll become, but rarely do those dreams come to pass exactly as we thought. And if we hang on to old hopes, bad decisions, or past injuries, that can steal our pleasure. Here are some ideas that will help you move beyond the past.

Visualize

If you think about how things should be or should have been, take a deep breath and visualize a box labeled *Expectations*, then mentally put those thoughts in that box.

Decide What's Important

Instead of thinking of all the things you'd like to say or do "if you only could," use your energy to make changes you really want, or let those desires go.

Take Responsibility

Growing up, whenever I came home upset about something, my mother would ask, "Where is your responsibility in this?" That always made me angry, but then I realized she was teaching me that when I focused on a perceived injustice rather than what I could have done differently, I was giving away my power.

Throw It Away

Emotional baggage is hard to throw away, but if you do, you'll find you have much more room to grow. Is there a memory causing you stress? Write it down and burn the pages. Physically removing a symbol of that emotional turmoil will help you move on to experience new pleasures.

Transform Your Narrative

Maybe you're still harboring bitterness toward a lover who hurt you. Instead of focusing on that pain, remind yourself that you'd never have recognized the positive traits in your current love if you hadn't gone through that experience.

FIND YOUR PLEASURE

THE SOUL OF OBJECTS

I was only six years old when my paternal grandmother passed away. I still remember fragments of her: her soft, ample bosom and raspy laugh. She was a fascinating, rebellious character—a woman who left her husband at a time when divorce was unpopular, who regularly traveled to Kenya to teach. My sister and I would often receive letters on paper decorated with photos of the most exotic butterflies we had ever seen, in which my grandmother shared stories of the giraffes and elephants she glimpsed out her bedroom window.

After the funeral, my family set up a table with a collection of her most precious objects. There was a family ring with delicate, colorful gemstones representing each of our birthdays, and various talismans and beaded artwork collected from her travels. Each of us took turns choosing items to keep. I carefully made my selections and created a small shrine in a drawer at home, regularly pulling out these items, as if they were Aladdin's lamp, hoping that if I touched them enough, she would reappear.

Objects possess a kind of soul; they contain memory, meaning, and—I believe—a bit of magic. They remind us of important people and faraway places. They can bring long-lost memories to life.

Pleasure Project

Make a time capsule for your family.
Make sure to include a message to your future self, too.

FIREWORKS

When I was a kid, we never bought our own fireworks. I'm not sure exactly why, but I'm certain my mother thought, *You can watch them down at the beach for free!* and my dad secretly worried that one of us would lose an eye.

My partner has none of those concerns. So for the past few years, he's brought home an array for us to set off in our yard with his father and our son.

I never expected this but *I love them*! They're loud and a tad obnoxious and the majority of them go off way past my bedtime, but when I manage to stay up, I find them utterly magical.

What is it about them that is so mesmerizing?

Scientists suggest these sudden, bright, moving sparks are so unusual to human eyes we're compelled to look at them. Other than fireflies and shooting stars, there's nothing else we see that looks anything like them.

These colorful, sparkly explosions are also a visual manifestation of our emotions. Think about it: when we fall in love, have great sex, can't hold back our tears, these are all explosions of our feelings. Some of these feelings are big and loud, some are tiny and sound like the beating of our hearts. All are unique.

There's something a little scary about fireworks, too. They're unpredictable, somewhat dangerous. And it's in that sweet spot between delight and fear that we find the dazzling pleasure of fireworks.

Home

FIND YOUR PLEASURE

MAKE YOUR HOUSE A HOME

Everyone who's ever traveled for any length of time knows the delicious sensation that washes over you when you return home—a feeling perhaps best described as comfort mixed with memory and meaning.

The essence of your soul tends to echo through your home. It's embedded in all the sensory choices you've made, and, as such, your home is as much a reflection of your relationship to pleasure as it is to your personal tastes.

So it's worth thinking deeply about the kinds of things you want to have in it. Perhaps you're a world traveler who collects keepsakes on your adventures, or maybe you have a few precious items from a loved one who's no longer with you. Or you're someone who's drawn to things that have no sentimental value but provide you with a feeling of calm and order—soft fabrics and natural materials like wood and stone.

Over the course of your relationship with your home, you'll likely have to transform your spaces from time to time to reflect your ever-changing style or family status. My house had a spare bedroom that I transformed into a tiny oasis where I could think and dance, but then my son came along and that spare room became his bedroom and its look evolved accordingly. After all, it's one thing to create a space that's a reflection of you and you alone; it's infinitely more challenging when there are lovers or little ones around!

Whatever the evolutions you face, the most important thing to remember is that the pleasure of a home isn't really about style or size or even the spaces themselves but about the memories people will create there.

My mother's garden is a place where magic lives. It's a bit like entering into a Monet painting. Everywhere you look there are splashes of gorgeous colors—bright pinks, soft purples, sunny yellows, and lush greens. You might also be lucky enough to spot a monarch butterfly, a bunny rabbit bouncing along, or one of her moonflowers opening right before your eyes.

Any gardener will tell you that the process of choosing the right plants and deciding where each will go is a lot like creating a work of art. Then there's the ritual of nurturing and watching things grow and transform over time, revealing all their glory. Gardens are like so many pleasurable things in life—they simply can't be rushed.

My mother loves her garden, rattling off the names of her flowers as if they were good friends and neighbors. When you think about it, plants *are* a lot like people. Some are tall, some are short. Some are quietly reserved, others simply burst with personality. Some smell lovely, others . . . not so much. Some get along wonderfully, others don't like to sleep in the same bed. Together, though, along with all the creatures that appear, they're not only beautiful, but they make up a complex and incredible world, with the plants themselves emitting the very oxygen we breathe.

Is it any wonder we adore everything about gardens? We literally need them to survive.

Pleasure Project

Plant a bee-friendly garden and pop pots of herbs and edible flowers
throughout. Or how about creating a guerrilla garden—scatter
seeds in your yard and see what comes up.

FIND YOUR PLEASURE

WONDER WALLS

When I was in university, I moved with a group of girlfriends into a classic Victorian house complete with high ceilings, stained-glass windows, and built-in mahogany bookshelves. Oh, how I wish I'd bought it! Yet despite its original beauty, the house was a little cobwebby and drab, which didn't feel like "us." So one of the first things we did was transform the walls.

The kitchen instantly became sunnier when it was painted a butter yellow; the dining room came to life with a passionate, deep shade of red; over a six-pack of beer, my boyfriend and I painted my room a moody shade of mauve that surely was inspired by my obsession with Prince. I put up a display shelf that featured a pair of sparkly antique shoes and hung up some 1950s-style bras that came from my days working at a vintage store. One of my roommates unearthed her favorite family photos and clipped them onto strings with brightly colored clothespins.

Walls can reflect our deeply personal stories. But no matter what you do, be fearless with your choices and have fun. After all, both the process and the result should be a joy. Below are some ideas.

- Chances are you have a friend or family member who is an amazing artist. Invest in their work. Or a search on Instagram will unearth an array of affordable, original art.

- There's something raw and honest about kids' art. So find a little person you love and get them to create something for you and frame it.

- If you have photos from various cameras (or eras), turn them all black-and-white.

- Collect different pieces of wood, or corks from wine bottles, and cover all or part of a wall.

Pleasure Project

Cover a wall with black chalkboard paint. You'll have a place to leave spontaneous love notes, and the dark color will make your room seem larger.

FIND YOUR PLEASURE

A MARRIAGE OF STYLES

Combining your decorating style with a partner's isn't always the easiest thing to do. Perhaps you like mid-century modern and your partner likes minimalism. Or you like Scandinavian and your partner prefers shabby chic. Don't worry—it's not time for a divorce—but if you share a space, you'll need to find a way to compromise.

First, collect images of interiors you love. Whenever my partner and I want to change something in our house, we each collect ten to twenty images. Then we compare those images to see where there are similarities or where the differences could complement one another. There is no shortage of magazines and apps that can help you do this, but I love Pinterest. If this doesn't feel like a pleasurable project to you, though, outsource it to stylish friends or experts.

When you've figured out what style you both gravitate to, pick one item each that is of such importance that you must have it on display. Maybe for you, it's a painting you bought after you landed your first big job; perhaps for your partner it's a treasured family heirloom. Find similarities in the two items—colors, shapes, materials, or textures—and then create the rest of your space by riffing off those unifying details.

If you manage to work in this way, you'll not only complement each other's style, hopefully you'll wind up complimenting each other while you're at it!

Once, I was on my way to a friend's house and decided to pick up a bouquet of peonies. While I was with her, the peonies opened up, their soft and fragrant petals exposing a deep red inside—it was like witnessing a big floral orgasm. What a treat!

Flowers are not only beautiful, they have a positive impact on well-being, too: researchers have found that their presence triggers happy emotions and heightens feelings of overall life satisfaction.

If you want something long-lasting, there's no shortage of plants you can use to enhance your space and add a sense of nature to your home. Choose an orchid— we have one that's been blooming on and off for five years, since we keep nurturing it. Or how about my new favorite: Succulents? What a delicious word for these little juicy and fleshy botanical wonders! They look adorable in tiny clay pots or as additions to larger glass terrariums. Or take advantage of views of greenery outside: merely glancing at shades of green can boost creativity and motivation.

Whatever your green fix, know that nature is a great way to deeply nurture your soul.

Pleasure Project

Instead of waiting for a friend or lover to buy you a bouquet of your favorite flowers, go out and treat yourself! There's something intensely satisfying about picking out your favorite flowers and arranging them by color and texture. You can also take some of the flowers out of the bouquet and separate them into tiny containers to scatter them throughout your home.

FIND YOUR PLEASURE

THE ZEN OF MESS

L ife is messy. Sometimes there are piles of laundry, and the bed isn't made. And there are days when dirty dishes are stacked in the sink and crumbs and sticky bits dot the counter.

While mess definitely can have a negative impact on mood, one of the biggest pleasure killers in life is obsessively focusing on this. I know so many women who will forgo sensual delights because they feel they need to clean up. Instead, remember that your path to bliss includes thinking about yourself and your needs—so when you need help, ask for it.

To start you off, here are useful ways to approach mess.

Reframe Things

Instead of seeing an unmade bed and getting upset, remind yourself of the wonderful sleep you had. When you come across a dirty sink, promise yourself a treat when you're finished cleaning it. Instead of despairing at the sight of dirty dishes, remember the wonderful meal you shared with a friend.

Set the Stage for Pleasure

Put on some music or a podcast you love, and allow your mind to wander as you clean. Or try to be fully present: feel the warm water as you wash dishes; focus on textures as you organize a closet.

Carve Out Space

Designate somewhere in your home that's yours and yours alone (see the Pleasure of Freedom on page 133 for more on this) that's always cleaned and organized as you like, so you can retreat there if things become overwhelming in other spaces.

Escape Outside

Go for a brisk walk. Nature can be cluttered and messy, and yet it's still beautiful—wild and ever changing. So instead of seeing your space as a chaotic disaster, view it as lush and alive—a potent reminder of all the other pleasurable things in life that you've been focusing on instead.

FIND YOUR PLEASURE

MOOD LIGHTING

When we were building our home, Jason focused a lot of time on making sure the lighting was just right. At first I thought that was silly, but now I understand the significant impact lighting can have. Soft lighting can make us feel quiet and peaceful. Bright lights can make us feel energized and awake. There are so many options available: pot lights on moody dimmer switches, beautiful lamps with colored light bulbs, sparkling twinkle lights, and more. It's important to consider the space the lighting will be going in: we tend to eat more slowly and consume less when lighting is soft, and there's no question that certain colors of light can set a mood—for instance, warm reds in the bedroom can help heat things up, if you know what I mean.

It's also amazing what a few candles can do. We've started to create a little ritual in our home around lighting a few beeswax candles whenever we have dinner, and our son absolutely loves it. It seems to set the stage for good conversation like nothing else.

I can't imagine how flat my home (and my life) would feel without all these pleasurable variations of light.

Pleasure Prompt

Ask the universe a question. Light a candle and listen carefully for a response.

MAKE SPACE FOR THE GOOD STUFF

A few years ago, I was on my way to a doctor's appointment on a drizzly, dark, windy day. I had my head tilted down while my umbrella half-assedly protected me from the elements. As I crossed a busy intersection, some guy beeped his horn at me. For a moment, I thought he was rushing me. But when I turned to look at him, I realized that he was pointing at the ground behind me.

There, smack dab in the middle of the intersection, was a bra. My bra. And not a sexy, lacy, black bra, either. No, it was one of those nude strapless things that may or may not have had breast-milk stains on it. I ran back, grabbed it, and shoved it in my purse.

This moment could have been—should have been—a wake-up call. The bra fell out of my purse because it was perpetually filled with too much crap. I've never been one of those women who can manage with a teeny, tiny purse. I've always carried my life around with me. I liked to think it was because if the zombie apocalypse hit I'd be fairly well prepared. But the truth was I just carried around too much crap. And I started to realize that shit was weighing me down, literally and figuratively.

Aside from the bra, the signs were obvious. Every time someone grabbed my bag, they inevitably said, "What the hell do you have in here? Rocks?" I also threw out my back, not once but twice in a year. I had to acknowledge that my overflowing purse was a visual manifestation of my cluttered, disorganized mind. So I opened up my bag and finally began unpacking.

Let go of the things that are weighing you down.

Like Allison's from *The Breakfast Club*, my purse was filled with everything from crinkled-up underwear to sad tampons to forgotten makeup to mysterious plastic bags. As I was emptying away, I felt like I was on *Let's Make a Deal*—except no one was going to give me any prizes for my stuff. I had to ask myself: What do these items say about me? Why am I afraid to get rid of them? Is it a fear of letting go of things I might need? Or just letting go?

But I did let go and since then, I've started looking at other places I can do the same thing. Maybe I don't need to hold on to my son's first everything, or I can lose that pair of pants I haven't fit into in years. And, less literally, maybe I can let go of the idea that when I gain a few pounds, I've somehow failed as a woman, or that if I make a single mistake at work, I don't really deserve my job.

We all carry around extra stuff. It might be pointless anger or bad habits, ridiculous expectations or negative self-talk. If any of this sounds like you, it's probably time to take that stuff out, look at it, and decide what you don't need anymore. Because when you let go of things that you don't want, you make room for what you need.

Pleasure Prompt

Give away things you no longer use or start a share program in your neighborhood.

FIND YOUR PLEASURE

TASTY DISHES

When a dear friend was getting married, the venue she chose didn't have dinnerware, so we visited a place that rented it. I remember watching her transform into Goldilocks while trying to select the right spoon. "This one is too small." "This one is too big." "This one is too round."

At the time I was stupefied as to how anyone could agonize over such a seemingly inconsequential thing. Surely no one at her wedding would even notice the subtle differences between spoons. Right? Wrong.

I've since come to realize that all the things we eat or drink with have a profound impact on how we experience meals, and that, just like my friend, I gravitate toward certain plates, spoons, and cups and avoid others. I have a set of glasses I hate drinking out of because of the way they're shaped. I even derive a degree of barbaric pleasure whenever one of them "accidentally" breaks. (There are only two left to go!) A mason jar glass, on the other hand, gives me a huge amount of pleasure.

I wonder about this connection between pleasure and what we use to consume things. Obviously the link starts right out of the womb. When I went back to work and was still breastfeeding my son, we tried out at least ten different bottles before he'd take my milk that way. He knew what he liked in his mouth, and not just any fake nipple was going to cut it. Then there are the things you love because you have a nostalgic attachment to them. That tea set that once belonged to your grandmother. Or the small silver baby spoon you secretly eat oatmeal with because it fills you with memories of your child doing the same.

Turns out there's another sort of connection. A group of researchers have found that cutlery and other dishes can change the way we perceive taste and add a sort of "seasoning" to food. Angular plates sharpen the bitter flavors of dark chocolate or coffee-flavored desserts, rounder dishes make things taste sweeter, cheese tastes saltier eaten off a knife, and yogurt seems yummier (and more expensive) when eaten with a silver spoon instead of a plastic one. So it turns out we do eat with our eyes first, in more ways than one!

As for those glasses I hate? I'm going to give them away—life is too short to bother with household items that don't make you feel good.

FIND YOUR PLEASURE

COZINESS OF THE SOUL

I love fall. The arrival of cooler breezes conjures up an indescribable feeling—the urge to pull on fluffy socks, sip wine or hot drinks with close friends, and cuddle under blankets by candle or firelight.

I don't have a word for it, but the Danish do. *Hygge.* Pronounced *HUE-gah*, it describes a feeling or the energy that comes from taking pleasure out of ordinary moments, or "warm, fuzzy, unpretentious moments," a "coziness of the soul," and "snuggly satisfaction." It may also be a distant cousin of the word *hug.* This unique outlook might be part of the reason that Denmark is listed as one of the world's happiest countries.

The wonderful thing is that *hygge* can be created anywhere—your home, your office, or your favorite coffee shop—so long as the people there have no agenda but are simply taking the time to just "be." Coziness is a big part of the feel, so choose throw pillows that make you swoon, cozy carpets for your feet, and towels that not only soak up water but also feel supersoft. When one of my friends was pregnant, she bought herself a deep, fluffy chair, with curved lines, appropriately named the womb chair. She spent the better part of the first year of motherhood nestled in it with her baby boy.

It's easy to get your *hygge* on. Whether it's making a coffee and brushing the cat as part of your morning ritual, snuggling under a warm throw for an afternoon nap, or lighting a candle as you get ready to have a quiet dinner party with friends, get into *hygge*ing.

Indulge Yourself

Find a cozy spot and reread a book you loved as a child.

ANIMAL LOVE

Have you ever thought about how pets—those unique souls—are named for the activity that brings us such mutual pleasure?

I didn't have pets as a kid, but my life changed when my first pet entered my life. We were doing renovations on our house, and a serious-looking Maine coon waltzed through our front door and sat on a ladder. He came and went for weeks—as if he were trying to see if we were right for him. Eventually, he never left. We called him Sally Hotdog, a name that suited this strange and sassy creature that loved to be held like a baby. I didn't yet understand the deep connection you can have with a pet, but Sally Hotdog showed me the way.

Anyone who's ever owned a pet realizes the impact they have on our well-being: the soothing feeling that comes when staring deeply into their eyes, the laughs they bring to our lives, and the way their mere presence in a home changes the energy of our spaces for the better. Even the non-cuddly animals we keep, like fish and lizards, seem to play a part in adding a sense of soul to a home. Many of us know someone who's been broken by heartache but then found hope and purpose again through their pets. Some pets even have a special sixth sense of a kind and are used as therapy animals to help those suffering from illness or trauma.

Ever since becoming a cat owner, I've learned some of the best life lessons from my cat:

Be unapologetically yourself.

Have cozy spots in your home to retreat to.

Know when to ask for cuddles—but don't be afraid to walk away when you've had enough.

Take a nap when sleepy.

Draw a bath when in doubt.

Whichever pet you may have, you can be sure they'll not only impart a great deal of knowledge but also provide you with unconditional love and untold pleasures as you share life together.

Parenting

FIND YOUR PLEASURE

THE WONDER OF PREGNANCY

The experience of being pregnant was life changing for me. I vividly remember that feeling of excitement mixed with apprehension when I peed on that stick and after a few minutes it magically showed me that little happy face. Was I happy? I wasn't sure at first.

But it didn't take long for me to melt into the wonder of it. Watching my body transform and feeling my senses expand, I began to feel like a curvaceous superhero. I got such pleasure from these little tweaks and pulls deep within my body—I sometimes felt as if this little being was sending me secret messages. It wasn't all pleasurable, though. I had bouts of unexplained bleeding. I ended up in the hospital, which led to a full-blown panic attack. I was certain I was going to lose this little person, and I had to rely on Jason and hope to get me through.

In the end I can look back and see that this process was preparing me for the incredible highs and lows that come with parenting something monumentally important.

Whether you become pregnant or not, a parent or not, there are many things we grow—ideas, insights, projects, relationships. There are nerves and apprehension, sickness, flutters of excitement, pain, and deep chasms of love. We have to simply sit back and trust in surviving the outcome—whatever it may be. If we do give birth to this creation of ours, we eventually have to let it separate from us, and wander around in the world alone.

The process is terrifying and makes us feel immensely vulnerable, but also reminds us of our untapped strengths. And that despite our best intentions, we are not—cannot be—in control of every aspect of these things we love so much. All we can do is rein in our expectations and trust in the experience. After all, what is life for if not to feel it *all*?

MILESTONES

Like a precious flower hidden away in a book, my memories of the early days of parenting are hard-pressed but softly faded.

I remember staring in amazement at my son's little fingers wrapped around one of my fingers. His tiny, birdlike mouth opening and closing, sending the message "Feed me." Tears, his and mine, and exhaustion like I had never felt before. But I also remember around six weeks in—when I thought I couldn't handle much more of anything—that this small boy looked up at me and smiled. That baby grin, that little tiny milestone, brought me a sense of pride and pleasure I had never known before.

After turning over that milestone, I kept looking for more. I marveled when he held his head up during tummy time, applauded when he turned over, stood in awe as he eventually pressed his small legs into the ground and held himself up. Then I listened as his sounds evolved into words. Every milestone hit was a marvel of how fast a microscopic being can become a little person with his own story and soul.

But in this world of micromanagement and competitive parenting, those childhood milestones can also easily and quickly become a source of stress. I remember so many mothers, including me, wondering if a milestone was happening at the right time and in the right way. Spurred on by parenting websites and the odd health-care provider, we sometimes scrutinize adorable things like animal noises and potty time instead of celebrating them.

Looking back, I can see that stressing about these things was such a waste of my time and energy. After all, unless there are other major problems, you can rest assured your child will go to university knowing how to count, brush their teeth, and wipe their bum properly.

So let every milestone—whenever it comes—be a source of magic and marvel in your life. As they say, the days are long, but the years are far too short.

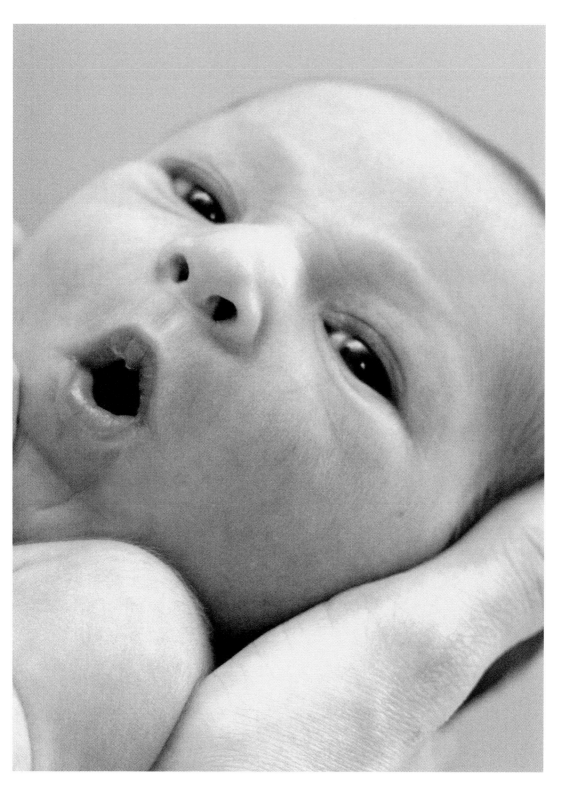

FIND YOUR PLEASURE

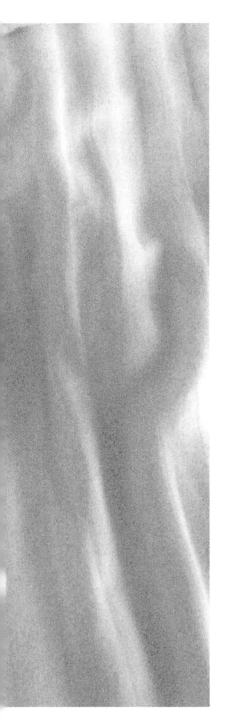

WHERE TO SLEEP

When you're a new parent, there's one question that's ever present: Where should the baby sleep? Some say cosleeping is the best. Others, that the baby should be in his or her own bed. The information out there is so contradictory, which makes the new world of parenting extra stressful.

Initially I planned to have our son sleep in our bed to make nursing easier. But I found he was such a wiggly worm that I was getting zero sleep, so I moved him into a bassinet at the end of the bed. But he rocked back and forth continually, which also kept us awake. (We *may* have had a few nights where he slept in his bassinet in the bathroom with the fan on—enough times that our fan doesn't work anymore.) Finally, after a few days of trying different things, we just moved him into his crib. He liked it. And *we liked it*!

All to say, there is no one right sleeping arrangement: Do whatever works for you. After all, you are never more aware of how pleasurable any amount of sleep is than when you become a parent.

FIND YOUR PLEASURE

THE JOYS OF NURSING

There are incredible benefits to breastfeeding. And I'm not talking just about benefits for your baby, but for you.

In recent years, though, breastfeeding has become highly politicized. But what if the conversation stopped being about what breast milk can do for the baby and whether you're a "good mom," and instead was about what breastfeeding can do for you? Because that's the thing no one told me about—the pleasure it would bring to *me*.

What kind of pleasure? Blissful oxytocin rushes, the power and confidence to soothe at any time in any occasion, weight loss . . . I could go on. I'm not gonna lie to you: The beginning was tough. And it can be really tough for some depending on latches, pain thresholds, and so on. It might be helpful to remember that just like any other goal we work toward, sometimes we need to go through some discomfort in order to reap the biggest rewards.

Some people have assumed that because I'm a breastfeeding advocate I must judge women who choose to formula feed. The truth is I judge people who don't give women the support, love, and encouragement they need, whatever choice they make. If something isn't pleasurable for you, then just stop. Guilt, mommy-shaming, and anxiety have no place in a life that is pleasure-focused.

Remember: Your body is a miraculous thing—in fact, the more that little bird nurses, the more milk your body will produce. Don't worry if it doesn't feel like he or she is getting enough—it's okay, Mama, breathe—as long as there are regular wet diapers and the little critter is growing, your tiny human is getting enough.

SNUGGLE UP

A newborn basically does nothing but eat, sleep, and shit. And they do that rotation a lot.

If you want to get anything else done, you're going to need a carrier. Whether it's something structured to wear on your back or just a long piece of fabric that you wrap around so that your little one is right next to your heart (or boob), a great carrier will save you. You'll love the cozy feeling of having your newborn snuggled close to you, and if it's a front-carrying one, you'll get to gaze at your baby all day.

Added bonus: your hands are free, so you can do other things, like go to the bathroom, make yourself lunch, look at a magazine, do some knitting, or any other enjoyable thing that strikes your fancy.

Indulge Yourself

Walk around a flower garden with your little one and see if you can spot a fairy.

FIND YOUR PLEASURE

RHYMING TIME

When my son first started eating solids, he loved them all—salmon, broccoli, chicken, steak, spinach. Then, as he discovered things like rice and pasta, those other things became increasingly less fun.

We tried sneaking heartier things in, but he sniffed out those healthy foods like a bloodhound. We started bargaining with him—not for dessert but for more food. Apparently, though, bargaining is a bad idea that can lead to overeating and unhealthy relationships with food. So I spoke with a doctor who said to teach kids this phrase: "One bite to be polite."

Our son now says and *does it* all the time.

Rhyming FTW!

Pleasure Prompt

Play with your food! Turn a pancake into a face with raspberry eyes. Or a sandwich into a dinosaur with carrot spikes. Do it for the kids in your life, your friends, or just for yourself.

FIND YOUR PLEASURE

UNEXPECTED GIFTS

We read a lot of Curious George stories in our house, and I've recently realized that in all of them, when George gets into trouble, the difficulty usually leads to something really lovely. The same is true in life.

When we took down the side of our son's crib to make it into a big-boy bed, we knew that we were making a scary transition. What sort of trouble would he get into? The answer? A lot! At first it was a nightmare, but once he adjusted, we received an amazing gift. Now, every morning, we wake up to the pitter-patter of little feet running down the hall to our bedroom and know that we'll soon be smothered in hugs and kisses.

And even though our little monkey still sometimes gets into mischief, we know that it's through the mistakes and messes of life that we learn the best lessons.

CAPTURING FEELINGS

When my son first started preschool, there were lots of tears. But his teachers had a system in place for such times; they would take the weeping student aside and ask them to dictate a letter, which invariably read something like this: "Dear Mommy, I am so sad I can't see you right now, please come back. I love you and miss you so much." The effect was remarkable. As soon as those thoughts were written down, the tears would dry up and the child could then go on with his or her day.

Research suggests that no matter what your age, there's something cathartic about the act of putting your feelings and experiences on paper. And it's a way of documenting the fine details of your life, which might otherwise be forgotten. There's also something magical that can happen when you make writing a habit—some of the deepest truths can come to the surface. (For more on this, see The Power of Journaling on page 192.)

So write things down with your child. If you don't know how to start, simply begin with these prompts.

I feel . . .

I know . . .

I wish . . .

I hope . . .

I love . . .

LEARN TO NEGOTIATE

I have, on more than one occasion, taken a crappy deal from an employer or a lover because I haven't asked for what I wanted. But my son has taught me how to be a better negotiator. When it's close to bedtime and he isn't ready to stop whatever he's doing, he comes up with a plan for bedtime. Watch a TV show, have a bath, then get into bed. Or have a bath, read stories, then get into bed. When he comes up with the idea, he is 99 percent more likely to stick to it.

There are two lessons here: First, if you're the negotiator, think of the outcome you want before going into negotiations. When you know what you want, then you can work backward to figure out the best strategy to achieve your desired results. Second, if you're the person dealing with the negotiator (could be an employee or child), it's important to remember that the more input the negotiator has and the more they feel heard, the happier and more helpful they will be.

In the end, negotiations can be a pleasure, not a pain. I promise!

REMEMBER YOUR CHILDHOOD

When I was a kid there was nothing I loved more than spending an afternoon drawing with a Spirograph, weaving God's eyes, or playing with Play-Doh. Guess what? All of that stuff still exists, and I'm much more dexterous now, so the possibilities for creating cool things are endless. With my son by my side, I've sewed puffy fabric cookies, made a felt mobile of stars and moons, and rediscovered the pleasure of doing puzzles. Even if you don't have kids, I highly recommend unearthing some of your childhood pleasures and taking a trip back in time.

Indulge Yourself

Play with some slime. Don't think about the mess, just indulge in the ooey-gooeyness of it. Or watch online clips of people playing with slime.

FIND YOUR PLEASURE

GET ON THE FLOOR

Whenever my son says, "Play with me!" and I don't feel like playing with trucks or LEGO, I just lie on the floor. He falls for it every time, and I get the advantage of two things: (1) I'm lying down and everything is better lying down, and (2) I can spend a great deal of time doing almost nothing and still absolutely delight him. One minute I'm a bucking bronco, then I'm a two-headed monster, then my hand is a sly snake looking for a little leg to curl around.

The possibilities are endless. You can wrestle, tickle, or hide under a blanket and play ghost. You can make a secret fort out of a couple of pillows and a chair and pretend to go to sleep. Sometimes, if you're really lucky, you might actually fall asleep.

FIND YOUR PLEASURE

SEEK OUT PLEASURE

One of the things that no one ever really described to me about having kids is the complete joy you get from watching your kids experience . . . life.

Kids are little pleasure lovers. They seek it out. Find it in the most unexpected places. Are devastated when it ends. There's something so raw, unbridled, and honest in their reactions to anything remotely fun.

I've watched my son experience extreme bliss while looking at a leaf and spend a ridiculous amount of time observing a bug. He is beyond delighted making creatures out of shells found on the beach. That attention and joy are reminders of how cynical, distracted, and uninspired at life adults often are. We ignore beauty and disregard magic. Living a sensual life requires a fierce and vibrant connection to imagination. Because this world is a beautiful, sensual, awe-inspiring place—if we pay attention.

Many of us have lost our sense of play. When was the last time you rolled around on the grass or in blankets for no reason? Or spent time contemplating the intricate beauty of sea creatures, or doodling in the snow? Dear reader, I'm going to do those things now. I suggest you join me.

Indulge Yourself

Since you spend more than half your life in your bed, make sure you choose the softest, coziest, and most sensual materials to wrap yourself in.

FIND YOUR PLEASURE

BIG BOX MAGIC

When you get something that comes in a big box, keep the box because it has special powers. You can draw on it and cut holes in it to transform the box into a rocket ship. Get inside and count down to blastoff. Where do you land? A whole new planet filled with strange aliens? Your box could be anything—a fancy picnic table, a buried treasure chest, a stuffed animal house, a ship to a faraway land. Take a page from your kid's book and tap into your imagination.

Pleasure Project

Playing dress-up isn't just for kids. There are entire communities of adults who regularly engage in cosplay. So whether you play dress-up while shopping (with or without the intention of ever buying), do it in the privacy of your bedroom to channel a different side of yourself, or create a full-blown costume of your favorite fictional character to wear to a fan event, let your imagination run free.

MAKE LEMONADE

A few years ago, I was driving up north with my son to visit my parents when we hit a spot of road construction. Traffic ground almost to a halt as concrete trucks and machinery moved at a glacial pace, and I began to worry that Jaya would complain about being in the car.

Then I heard him say, "Mommy, look at those trucks. What do you think they're building?" His sense of wonder was contagious, and soon enough, I started enjoying watching the trucks, too. That led to a game of "I spy . . . ," and the trip quickly went from being a sour lemon to delicious lemonade.

FIND YOUR PLEASURE

THE WISDOM OF CHILDREN

When you become a parent, people give you all kinds of lovely tips on how to capture your child's important moments: things like making a milestone book for your baby or saving a lock of hair from your child's first haircut in a small envelope taped behind your favorite photograph of him or her.

On the advice of a friend, I began keeping a notebook to write down all the funny and weird things my son said. Whenever I read it, I'm amazed at the wisdom in my son's words. Here are some of my favorites.

"One day, can you put me inside Daddy's head? He knows a lot."

"Maybe when we die that's when other people can live. It's like the dinosaurs—they died, we live."

"Hey! The sky looks like the ocean."

"You know why we sleep the same way? Because I am half you and you are half me."

The pleasure of a notebook like this is the joy it brings when you're creating it and looking at it years later, and the tiny glimpse it will give your child into who he or she used to be.

Pleasure Prompt

Take a walk with a dog or a child in the forest and go where they go. Get down to their level and try to see things from their point of view.

Love

Love
Yourself

BODY LOVE

Ewww. *Ugh. WTF is that?* Those are some of the things I've said to myself when looking in the mirror. It makes me feel like a jerk—I would never allow anyone to talk to themselves the way my inner voice often talks to me. Sure, I've gained weight over time. But instead of celebrating the decadent meals I've shared with friends and the wonderful time I've spent with my son and working on creative things instead of working out, I've been mentally flogging myself.

Like lots of people, I've been hard on my body for a long time. I come from a line of women who are hypercritical of themselves. I've watched my mother getting dressed and *tsk-tsk*ing her own reflection. She once told me that when she was around twelve, she was teased mercilessly by classmates when she returned home ten pounds heavier after a delightful summer with her *nonna* and *nonno*. I'm sure that was part of the reason she was so concerned about my body and my sister's as we were growing up. But that concern often felt like judgment. I also remember my gramma remarking on how beautiful certain women's bodies were and how some were just . . . not.

In so many families, thinness represents not only beauty but self-control, a quality envied in women. And gaining weight is a sin—with a particular kind of shame attached to overindulgence. Even little girls absorb these sorts of messages, so it shouldn't come as a surprise that eating disorders are prevalent among women, and that diets are all about restraint and restriction.

Even so, when I was young, I didn't think much about my body. I hopped in and out of bathing suits and felt fairly comfortable hanging out naked in my house. But then came puberty and an explosion of hair, cellulite, stretch marks, and shame. That shame translated into the bedroom. During my late teens/early twenties, not only did I feel unworthy of certain types of guys, I also put up with lackluster sexual encounters because of a severe lack of body confidence.

Every body is perfect.

Then I started hanging out with performers, and not just any performers. I remember the first time I saw a belly dancer. As soon as the music started, this shy woman went from looking down at the ground to staring at the audience as if to say, "Look at me!" The connection between the music and her curvy body was undeniable—it was as if the instruments were playing out of her pores. The effect was devastatingly sexy.

Later, I was a producer on a documentary series and had to be on a porn set. It was surreal, but I was struck by how comfortable the performers were wandering around completely naked. It didn't matter if they had cellulite, or the occasional stray hair—they acted as if there was nothing a little spray tan couldn't fix. Shortly after that, I interviewed burlesque performer, actress, and comedian Selene Luna, who, at three foot ten, may be a small package but has a big, sexy, and confident presence. More recently I've become deeply intoxicated by the wit and charm of transgender artist Vivek Shraya, who embraces hairy legs and winged eyeliner at the same time, refusing to conform to one single beauty standard.

Through these diverse interactions and experiences, I gained a new perspective, and my relationship to my body began to change. I learned to feel comfortable with it again. I also learned that there's no single definition of perfect—*everything* is perfect, and the only sure thing about our bodies is that they're always changing.

So what if you have spider veins? Or rogue hairs? When my sister and I were little, we'd sometimes lie in my mother's bed and play with the loose skin under her arms. She'd shoo us away—she felt ashamed. But we loved that it *felt* good. Imagine if you looked at your body through *that* lens. In a world that's filled with messages telling women how they should look, embracing ourselves, just as we are, is a deeply radical act.

So whenever I start sinking into self-loathing, I remind myself of the following:

This body gets me up out of bed every morning.

This body gives me the ability to move.

This body strokes my son's head and feeds him.

This body allows me to think, to create.

This body gives and receives pleasure.

What will you do today to appreciate *your* body?

FIND YOUR PLEASURE

THE POWER OF YES AND NO

How many times have you said an enthusiastic *yes* or *no* this week? How did it feel? Good, right?

When you know what you want out of life, when your eyes are focused on the prize of your big life goals, it becomes easier to say yes or no because each decision you make is inching you toward that.

When television producer, screenwriter, and author Shonda Rhimes embarked on a yearlong journey of saying yes, it was after years of being a self-described "no" person. "No" to that event. "No" to that invitation. "No, no, no" to that interview. She realized that saying no was a mechanism for self-protection, that she was afraid of the possibilities of yes—she didn't feel worthy of them. As she began saying yes, all kinds of worlds of pleasure opened up to her. The project led to a sense of self-acceptance, compassion, and love, which, despite all of her successes, she hadn't found till then.

Practice enthusiastic yeses and nos. Get good at asking for what you want and saying no to things that move you away from your goals. And if you don't know what to do, give yourself permission to say, "I'll get back to you," then consider if your yes or no will be a stepping-stone or a roadblock.

When you say yes to the things you love—that feed your soul, bring you deep pleasure, even sometimes scare you—you move through life buoyed by self-knowledge and confidence, and are better able to weather the storms that inevitably arise.

FIND YOUR PLEASURE

THE PLEASURE OF TOUCH

I'm in a room, lying on a bed completely naked, covered only with a thin sheet. I'm not alone. A fully clothed stranger is giving me a rubdown. I have paid this stranger quite a sum of money to cover me in fancy oils and warming lotions. Basically, to give me pleasure. This isn't a sexual exchange but a therapeutic one.

Do you ever wonder why we pay virtual strangers to massage our naked bodies? Because we crave touch.

Touch is arguably one of the most important and yet overlooked senses. Every second of every day, we receive tactile information about the world around us. Check in with your own touch sensations right now. Are you holding a book? A tablet? What does it feel like? Is it soft or hard? Cool or warm? What about where you're sitting? Does it feel cozy or rigid? You're touching all kinds of things, although you probably weren't even thinking of those sensations until you purposefully tuned into them.

Of course, we also touch other people. Think of the last person you touched—was it a firm handshake with a colleague? A warm hug from a friend? A knee-melting kiss from a lover? How long ago was it? If you can't remember, you're probably suffering from a touch deficit. We need touch to survive. Every person who has had a child recently knows that one of the first things they tell you in the hospital is the importance of skin-to-skin contact. Even if babies are given all the milk in the world, they simply won't thrive without the magical power of touch.

In our world, where people are more likely to be connecting through screens instead of sensations, never forget that we humans need to touch and be touched in the right kinds of ways in order to get the most pleasure out of life.

Pleasure Prompt

Touch yourself: rub your eyes, scratch your back, tickle your arms. Now keep going. Let pleasure be your guide.

BEST BATH

Baths are a near-universal pleasure. They're kind of like a liquid hug, aren't they? I often wonder if we love them because the sensations and warmth connect us to deep-seated memories of being in the womb. But I also think it's because baths are connected to other pleasures like privacy, sensuality, and relaxation, and they ultimately reconnect us with the quieter and softer parts of ourselves. Here's how to create the perfect one.

Set the Temperature

Too hot and you run the risk of feeling like you're having a hot flash. Too cool and you'll feel like you're in the tiniest lake.

Set the Mood

I like bright sunlight coming into the bathroom in the morning, and the flickering light of candles during the evening. Add good music or a great book.

Have a Drink

If you're having a morning bath, choose tea or coffee or perhaps lemon and water. If it's an evening bath, a glass of wine would be my drink of choice.

Add an Enhancer

Whether it's an essential oil spray, bath bomb, or bubbles, there's immense joy to be had in changing the way a bath smells or feels. Consider adult waterproof toys to take your pleasures to a whole other level.

FIND YOUR PLEASURE

THE ART OF SELF-SEDUCTION

Esther Perel is a brilliant marital therapist who often counsels couples struggling in the aftermath of an affair. She's noticed that people who enter into affairs often talk about an incredible feeling of being alive again, as if they've gone from sleepwalking to noticing every tiny beautiful thing in the world.

What if you could conjure that kind of seductive spell without an affair? If you set aside time to explore, provoke, and celebrate your body and mind with the care and attention that you'd give a new lover? I believe that, as important as our relationships are with our partners, friends, and families, recognizing that the longest relationship you'll ever have is with yourself is essential. If you don't stoke the fires of your own heart, you'll begin to lose touch with the magic of the world.

If I were to teach a course on self-seduction, I'd include the following rules:

- You are responsible for your own pleasure, sexual or otherwise.

- Before hopping into bed with anyone, you must hop into bed countless times with yourself.

- Explore the geography of your own landscape, internal and external. If there's something you want to change, first change the way you perceive it. So instead of lamenting the loss of muscle tone, appreciate the softness of flesh, or instead of focusing on stretch marks, see reminders of the journey of your life.

- Flirt passionately with nature, wild animals, and even other humans—in safe and respectful ways.

While Hollywood continues to sell a vision of romance as roses, sunsets, and happily ever after, the reality of love and life will always be much more complicated. Instead of being disappointed by that, cultivate safe forms of seduction wherever possible. Consider this your permission slip. Invoke the gods and goddesses of seduction—the Aphrodites and the Casanovas—and channel all that energy inward toward every curve and crevice, dimple and divot, bump and blemish.

In other words, love yourself, just as you are.

THE PULL OF WATER

The city I live in has a wonderfully long sandy beach. During each season you can find people there indulging themselves: a young couple reading with their legs intertwined, a topless Sophia Loren look-alike enjoying an ice cream, hijab-wearing mamas playing with their giggling babies, gay couples holding hands and walking their dogs. All these people from different worlds are brought together by one shared interest: to be near the water.

Something about water calls to us. What is it? Is it that we see ourselves reflected in it? That we are made up to a large extent of water? Does the sound of waves lapping on the shore remind us of the sounds we heard in the womb? Is it because all living creatures are so utterly dependent on water for survival that to be far away from it is unnerving?

I don't know the answers, but I do know that for me and probably you, too, water brings great and profound pleasure.

So if you're wondering about how to get more enjoyment out of life, think water! You can bathe in it to relax your body, swim in it to feel invigorated, drink it to quench your thirst, and listen to sounds of it to soothe yourself. Research has even found that people who fall asleep listening to sounds like rushing water or rain not only sleep more deeply, but their memories are boosted by the experience.

Whatever your connection to water, it is a powerful force that you can use to calm and refresh every part of yourself.

W e live in a time during which, if you have the funds, you can change any-thing you don't like about yourself. You can tweak, exaggerate, reduce, alter, and rearrange anything you choose—it's the age of bespoke bodies.

I support women's rights to do whatever they want to their anatomy. What concerns me are the endless possible things that could be lost. Do you ever won-der if, when we buy into a trendy idea of beauty, we're trading in the charm of individuality for the mundaneness of ubiquity? Or that we're exchanging our po-tential for pleasure for the promise of "pretty"?

If you look around, every wealthy white millennial seems to be sporting the bee-stung lip look. Back when I was growing up, everyone wanted superthin lips. My fuller lips were the source of endless insensitive probing and teasing. If you'd asked me at the time if I wanted a reduction, I might have said yes. But I adore my lips just as they are.

And the lips on our faces are just one thing. According to the American So-ciety of Aesthetic Plastic Surgery, the number of girls aged eighteen and under undergoing cosmetic surgical labial reconstruction or labiaplasty has nearly dou-bled between 2014 and 2015.

I find this incredibly troubling.

Like every part of our body, our genitals are distinctive. Some are long, some are short, some are pink, some are brown, some look like flowers, others like exotic sea creatures. The uniqueness is profound. But what all vulvas have in common is that, left as they are, they have the capacity to deliver incredible amounts of pleasure.

Celebrate all your incredible parts.

It's important to note that the epicen-ter of that pleasure is the clitoris, which is like the Beyoncé of our anatomy—beautiful, hardworking, and strong with an air of mys-tery. It's also a complex organ with at least eighteen distinct interacting func-tional parts—and what you see is only the tip of the iceberg. Why is that important to know? Because research shows that when young women under-stand how their bodies work, that empowers them to take more control of their pleasure.

And our bodies' potential for pleasure is, to me, what we should be focus-ing on.

All trends come and go. But our bodies? We have them for life.

So what if instead of altering ourselves in ways that we can never come back from, we chose to alter our perceptions? What if instead of encouraging women to feel insecure about a part of their body, we celebrated the diversity of all our incredible parts? What if instead of focusing on how they look, we revered the incredibly sacred and wild pleasures they can provide?

I promise you this, my friends, honor thy vulva and it will honor you back.

Indulge Yourself

Use your detachable showerhead to spray warm water everywhere on your body. Let it linger on the places it feels best.

TAKE A TIME OUT

If you're a parent, you know the power of giving your child a time-out. Whether they're overtired or "hangry" or going through a phase, sometimes kids need a moment alone to calm down. What I've recently discovered is that time-outs are good for us adults, too.

One day, I came home and the house was a mess. I'd planned on doing some work, but my son wanted my attention. It felt like every two seconds he was asking for something else. Finally, after dinner and dishes and playtime and bath and toothbrushing and stories—God, I get tired just writing that!—I put him to bed and promptly fell facedown into my own bed, only to be woken up hours later to his screaming, "Mommy! Come here!"

I shot out of bed and barreled down the hall, heart racing, thinking the worst. I threw on the light and said. "What's going on?!"

"I can't find my pillow!" he replied.

Guess where it was? Right under his head.

I lost it. I yelled at my poor son, and then I unloaded my anger on my poor partner who was innocently working in the basement and didn't hear a thing. Then I went upstairs and wept. The next morning, my partner booked me into a hotel for a much-needed break.

All of a sudden, my time was my own. I meandered. I sat at a bar and eavesdropped. I watched *Jeopardy!* (and solidified my knowledge that I will *never* be on that show). I drank wine. I ordered room service. I went for a swim. I took a *super*long shower. No one asked me for anything. No one woke me up. And the next day, I felt completely rejuvenated.

That is the power and pleasure of a time-out. I encourage you to take the money you might spend on a pair of shoes or a fancy dinner out and give yourself a night off alone. If that's not doable, try to schedule your own downtime to recharge even if it's just for a half an hour. Whether you're taking a break from technology, your work, or your family, it will not only help you de-stress, but will boost your creativity and passion.

Is it actually possible to have a pleasure-filled childbirth?" That was the question at the top of my mind when I got pregnant. In fact, one of the reasons I put off getting pregnant for so long was my abject fear of the pain of childbirth.

So when I stumbled across a series of videos online titled, "Orgasmic Birth," I thought, *Sign me the hell up!!* These videos were filled with women simply sighing their babies into being. Instead of the animalistic howls of pain I'd seen in countless Hollywood movies, they were making almost sensual sounds, radiating a distinctly calm glow.

Naturally, one of the first things I did was google *Orgasm + Birth + Classes*. Although I didn't find any promising orgasms in my neighborhood, I did find classes on hypnobirthing, which at least suggested a possibly pleasurable birthing experience. I promptly took them.

Inspired by midwifery guru Ina May Gaskin, the idea behind hypnobirthing is that when you're afraid, your entire body becomes tense, which only makes childbirth more painful. However, if you practice calming your mind through breath and visualization, your body follows, making birth less painful, possibly even pleasurable.

While I will not say that my son's birth was pain-free, I will say there were moments of sublime pleasure.

So is pain merely a state of mind?

Research has shown that it might be. And after all, we know that there are many instances of pleasure and pain overlapping. Think of the endorphins you receive during an intense workout. The thrill that comes from watching a scary movie or going on a roller coaster. Perhaps you relish that peculiar pleasure that comes from the burn of wasabi while eating sushi. Speaking of peculiar, how about the unique pleasure that comes from slowly squeezing a pimple? Yoga is often torture, until the release, and then it's pure pleasure. Or how about the pleasure that some receive from indulging in a few shades of "grey" in the bedroom?

Pain can transform into pleasure.

In other words, pain under the right circumstances, with the right mind-set, can transform into pleasure.

Yet we are a pain-averse society. Our focus on happiness and obsession with self-help teaches us to avoid pain and discomfort. Everywhere you look, we're being pushed pills or other remedies to mask or mute emotional and physical pain.

I believe that avoidance of pain has a cost. Without some pain in life, all of its pleasures might never be as sweet. And when you work through discomforts, embrace certain kinds of hurt, or even endure painful moments, you will uncover hidden pleasures.

Indulge Yourself

Slowly pluck a chin or boob hair and savor the peculiar delight that comes from pleasure mixed with a small dose of pain.

FIND YOUR PLEASURE

GETTING DRESSED

There was a time when I treasured the creative act of putting on different pieces from my wardrobe and prancing around in front of my mirror before confidently sashaying out the door. Since having my son, though, I've found dressing in the morning more than a bit of a pain in the ass. Right after childbirth, I developed some standard go-to outfits, but they did nothing to inspire me.

Recently, though, I've been trying to reconnect to this pleasure. This is my simple approach to clothes now: I only choose things that bring me deep pleasure. After all, anything that gets that close to our skin should not only be dazzling to the eye but also make us feel really sensual. With a bit of courage and a dash of hedonism, you, too, can turn the act of dressing or undressing into a pure delight.

Indulge Yourself

Take your bra and/or pants off at the end of a long day and acknowledge how much your mood improves.

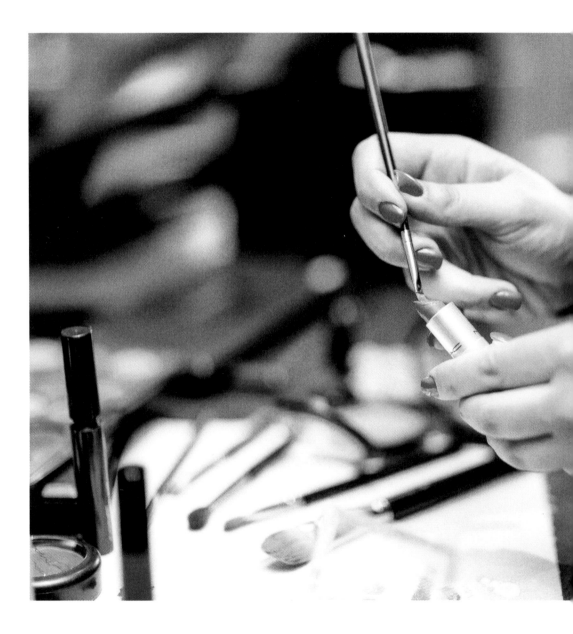

FIND YOUR PLEASURE

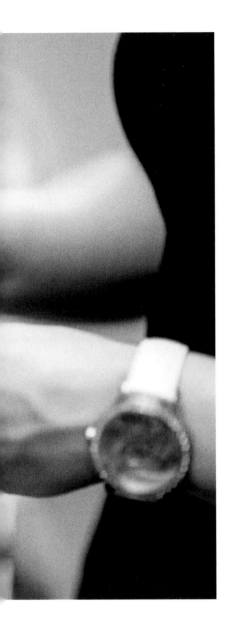

When I was a child, I'd secretly go through my mother's purse and take out her lipsticks, remove the shiny golden caps, and twirl the bottoms to reveal shades of crimson, fuchsia, and peach. The heavy, waxy smell mixed with the scent of leather from her purse said "woman" to me. Occasionally I would even dare to put some on before quickly wiping off the evidence. Even then I knew the power of a good lipstick.

I first wore lipstick in public when I was twelve. A friend and I were going to see a movie and decided to wear makeup in case we ran into some boys. She pulled a plastic strawberry compact that concealed pinky-coral glosses smelling of fruit and candy out of her bag, and we painted our lips and headed to a matinee of *Stand by Me*. Suffice it to say, there were no back-row make-outs that day, but damn we looked good!

Even during my earthy, hippie phase, I still couldn't give up lipstick. The simple act of putting it on, pressing my lips together, and being able to taste them felt sexy and empowering. Just what is it about lipstick? Why does it give such pleasure and a boost of confidence?

Anthropologist Desmond Morris believes one of the reasons we add color to our lips could be to remind potential lovers of the look of aroused genitals. When I got my first Chanel red, I'm not sure I felt like I was showing my arousal on my face, but since then I always have a few erotic shades in my purse, which never fails to provide quiet, secret surges of delight.

FIND YOUR PLEASURE

BODY MESSAGES

At one point, my back simply gave up. It had been giving me warnings—a little discomfort here, a little pain there—but I kept picking up my increasingly heavy toddler and wearing bad shoes, "too busy" to go to Pilates classes to strengthen my core or even to find the time to stretch. So what did my back do? It took me down.

Our bodies are wise. They hold stories locked up behind hidden doors deep within us. Sometimes those stories try to break free. At first they just knock. Maybe ring a soft bell. But eventually, if they aren't listened to, like little children they burst through the barriers we've built and demand our attention.

Arianna Huffington knows this firsthand. She was once so tired at work that she passed out—hitting her face on her desk so hard she required stitches. It was literally a wake-up call for her—she was burning out, and her life needed to change. She began to scale back on the amount of work she was doing, instituted a nap policy at work, and then even stepped down from her role at *The Huffington Post* to focus on her wellness brand.

Our bodies have so many ways of communicating with us—besides emotional breakdowns or burnout, there are things like irritable bowel syndrome, itchy skin rashes, or chest pain caused by acute stress. I'm not saying that all pain is some kind of manifestation of emotional issues. Sometimes shit just happens. But I think we would all do well to listen to the aches, pains, and emotions in our bodies and recognize if we're numbing, dulling, or trying to ignore them.

Whether you are really sick or in pain, or just tired, one of the messages your body is sending is to slow down. When my back gave up, I panicked at first, thinking, *There's so much that has to get done!* But even then, somehow, the important stuff got done. And the rest, it turned out, simply wasn't that important.

Pleasure Project

Write down everything you must do in a day. Decide which things you can ignore. Decide which things you can delegate. Recognize how the idea of simply passing stuff off makes you feel.

THE OTHER SIDE OF "SHOULD"

Picture this: You've had a long, tiring day and are finally able to curl up with a great book and a glass of your favorite wine. Instead of savoring this small pleasure, your brain suddenly goes, "I should be cleaning," or worse, "I should have hit the gym today."

Or you're sitting at home with your tantrumy child and see a neighbor driving off to work, and think, *I should be with adults right now!* Or you see a mama with a toddler in one hand and a baby strapped to her chest and you wonder, *Should I have another one?* Or you're driving through the country, past lush swaths of land and large houses, and you think, *I should move out of the city*, and you're suddenly sinking into an abyss of should'ves.

We women have a peculiar obsession with *should*.

The problem with *should* is that you never actually appreciate where you are and what you have. And the truth is there is always a trade-off. Because I know that for sure if I was living out in the country there would be moments when I would be screaming, "Holy crap, get me back to the city!"

Our lives aren't meant to be perfect. In fact, there really is no "perfect." The beauty of life comes from its unruliness, and the joy in living comes from looking around and noticing all the gifts life's unpredictable journey has brought you.

In other words, there is an incredible pleasure that comes from realizing that the place you're standing right now is exactly where you should be.

Indulge Yourself

Watch cat or dog videos. It isn't just a casual pleasure—it actually improves happiness levels. My fave? Maru the Cat trying to fit his juicy fluffiness into something.

Dating & Relationships

FIND YOUR PLEASURE

THE SWEETNESS OF KISSES

Even at their worst, I find kisses to be one of life's sweetest pleasures. It's an exchange. A dance. An incredibly intimate gesture.

My very first kiss was with a poster of River Phoenix on my bedroom wall. For the record, River did not reciprocate. My first kiss with a living, breathing human was in the hallway of my Catholic school. I was eleven. He was an overconfident, curly-haired Italian boy. The kiss was soft and gentle, but firm, and made my legs turn to water.

There have been many other kisses since—weird ones with guys with braces and aggressive tongues, great ones in the backs of cabs after too many glasses of Shiraz. My favorite kiss was right out in the open in a bustling downtown hot spot—you know who you are.

Have you ever wondered why we kiss? Some theorize that kissing evolved from the primitive practice of mothers chewing their food for their young and then feeding them mouth to mouth. Others think we kiss as a way to figure out if someone is a good biological fit for us.

I think it has to do with pleasure. Our lips are densely populated with sensory neurons, and when we kiss, they send messages to our brains, releasing a chemical cocktail that sets off a cascade of pleasurable sensations. That's why the first stage of love feels so addictive—and why first kisses and best kisses are among many people's most detailed memories.

Indulge Yourself

Kiss your lover in a way you never have before. Play with pacing, intensity, rhythm, location. Ask him or her to mirror your kisses exactly.

MAKE A DATE

Dating can be overwhelming. But there's so much pleasure to be had if you approach dating with the right mind-set. That thrill of hitting it off with someone new, those long, late-night conversations, those first touches. Here are tips for maximizing your pleasure while dating.

Keep Your Eyes Open

Time to get your flirting radar running again! Whether you're at work, the grocery store, or walking down the street, look at the people around you. Is there someone you find attractive? Are they looking at you? Direct eye contact and leaning in are great cues that someone is interested in you, but you won't notice any of that if you wander around with your lovely face buried in your phone.

Go Online

Try online dating. You can sit in your pajamas and filter through profiles until you see someone you like. The trick is volume. You don't have to go out with every Tom, Dick, or Harriet, but be willing to chat with a few people and, if you're gelling with someone, meet him or her for a coffee or lunch to see if there's passion in person.

Ask Questions

In her 2015 *New York Times* essay, "To Fall in Love With Anyone, Do This," Mandy Len Catron unearthed a 1960s research project that psychologist Arthur Aron conducted. He claimed that thirty-six questions could help foster intimacy between strangers. While they may not guarantee everlasting love, they'll help weed out mismatches. Here are a couple of examples: What constitutes a perfect day for you? When did you last cry in front of another person?

When we approach dating with curiosity and playfulness, the entire experience becomes infinitely more pleasurable. And while you're out there dating other people, don't forget to continue to romance yourself.

SIGNS YOU'RE WITH THE RIGHT PERSON

I've been in the same relationship for almost twenty years. I still look at him and wonder at the magic that brought us together. I'd be lying if I said it's been all sunshine over the years—we've definitely had tough times. But despite those challenges, there is no doubt in my mind that he is a great one for me. Notice that I didn't say "the one"—I think that idea is a load of crap. Imagine if your "one" was born in another part of the world? Or another century? How awful! But I do think there are a handful of people we may come across in our lives who are good fits for our unique quirks.

Here are some ways to know if the person you're with is right for you.

You Know Yourself

You, my friend, like everyone else, are imperfect. You have your own unique genetic makeup and personal history that has contributed to the person you are, and you're willing to own up to your shortcomings and mistakes. You've learned how to communicate in reasonable ways, and you expect the same from your partner. You also know your value and understand that your pleasure isn't dependent on another person, but entirely rests on your own shoulders. Whomever you choose to be with will be a complement, not a necessity.

You've Kissed a Lot of Amphibians

Maybe it's a few frogs, toads, or even a sal-amander or two. You paid close attention to what those different types brought out in you: Your confidence or your insecurities, jealousy or trustfulness, calm or unease. You've learned from your mistakes and know what works and what doesn't for you, and now can recognize someone of worth.

You Enjoy Intimacy Together

You know your body and what's good for you, feel safe exchanging ideas about pleasure, and aren't performing for your partner's pleasure. You and your partner recognize that sex will ebb and flow throughout a long-term relationship and know how to create intimacy beyond sex.

You Share Values

I know a couple who have been together hap-pily for more than twenty-five years. She's Palestinian and he's Jewish—they're basically a microcosm of world peace. They listen and communicate well and aren't rooted in a need to be right at all times. Take a page from their book and sort out whether you're on the same page when it comes to certain topics—religion, children, circumcision, vaccinations, abortion, equal rights, and money are a few that come to mind. It's best to have these talks sooner rather than later.

You Realize the World Isn't Black-and-White

Nor is it fifty shades of gray. In fact, it's a spectrum of colors. The world is complex and can bring joy and pain, and you may be confronted with challenges that can't be foreseen. If you're open, you won't make ultimatums or run away from confrontations. Ultimately, you're both confident that you can face any challenges with your partner in an empathetic and carefully considered way.

You Bring Each Other Pleasure

Relationships should add something meaningful to your life, not make you feel sad, unheard, lonely, or angry. All relationships go through times when you don't delight each other as much, but as long as the good consistently outweighs the bad, you're doing something right.

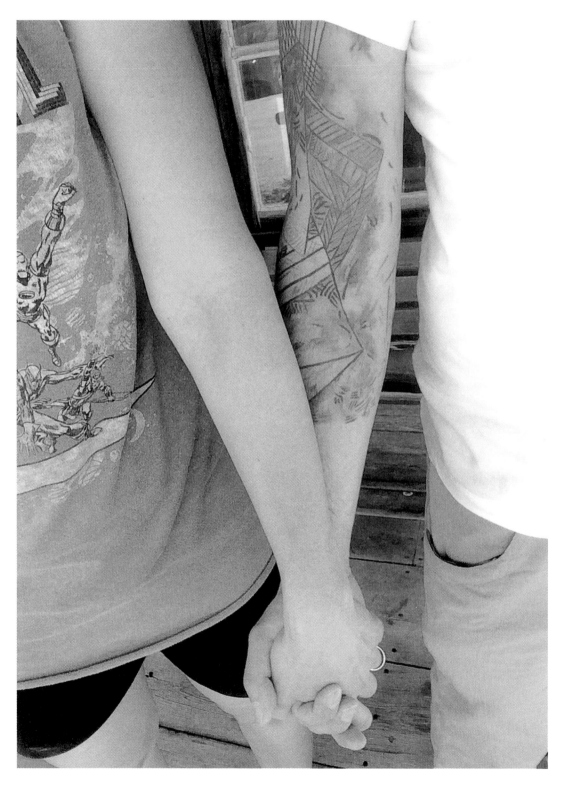

FIND YOUR PLEASURE

THE ALLURE OF CHAMPAGNE

L egend has it that on the night champagne was invented, a French monk named Dom Pérignon took a sip and ran outside, declaring to anyone listening: "Come quickly! I am drinking the stars!" Chances are this story was invented on Madison Avenue. But the image is so evocative, who cares?

For most of us, champagne is the first alcohol we ever taste, and so it leaves a distinct (often headachy) impression on us. But when champagne is done right, it can taste like living sparkles.

Allow me to tell you how I fell in love with champagne. My lover and I were going through a dark period. I was working a job I hated. Instead of doing all the right things to get back on track in a healthy way, I found myself starting to smoke again, staying out late, getting totally distracted by superficial pleasures. Eventually it all came to a head. My lover and I exchanged emails. I could feel the air between us warming up. I met with him and instead of retreading sensitive territory of more apologies, of trying to reason it all out, we pulled out a bottle of champagne and drew a bath.

Can I just point out that the entire process of experiencing champagne is so . . . sexual?

You delicately undress the cap. Gingerly take off the wire bra. Finally, you gently coax the cork back and forth until *pop*, it explodes in delight. Then, you pour the champagne into a flute and bring it to your lips. The liquid slides into your mouth, and citrusy, tingly, pearly notes dance on your tongue . . .

The rest of this story will have to go down in the secret annals of make-up sex. But to this day whenever champagne touches my lips, I always remember the night we drank the stars.

Indulge Yourself

Keep a bottle of something fancy in your fridge. You never know when a special occasion will arise.

FIND YOUR PLEASURE

PLEASURE OF FREEDOM

We all want freedom—freedom of thought, of movement, of opinion—but we also want commitment and stability, especially in our relationships. When we first start dating someone we like, we don't think too much about freedom because our feelings are so intense. It's as if we want to climb inside the other person. Eventually, though, after we've been together for a while and feel secure and well loved, we begin to crave separateness again. If we ignore that desire, resentment can build and pull us away from our partner. So how can we have both freedom and commitment?

Marital therapist Esther Perel says that "desire needs space to thrive." In other words, when you take time away from your partner, you give yourself the opportunity to crave closeness. A bit of space also creates mystery. Studies show that people in long-term relationships are most drawn toward their partner when they're able to see them at a distance, outside the routines of their relationship. Maybe it's watching them excel at their job, take up a new hobby, or playing with your child. Maybe it's trying out new things within the relationship, like going to an art show or a new restaurant.

One of the easiest ways to create a sense of freedom is to establish your own space (whether that's a corner in your basement, a spare bedroom, or in the garden), where you can escape and scream, cry, think, or fantasize in privacy, or have a set amount of time to yourself—a weekend of your own every couple of months, perhaps.

A little space can go a long way in creating desire within your relationship. There is so much pleasure to be found in freedom, and you just might find that you can't wait to share your adventures with your loved ones back home.

Pleasure Prompt

Take the time to look at yourself naked in the mirror. Write down three things you love about yourself.

GETTING OVER HEARTBREAK

As much as the entertainment industry wants us to believe that true love lasts forever and ever till the music swells and things fade to black and the curtain drops, the fact is, sometimes things fall apart. Relationships end. Divorce happens. There's no formula for "getting over" someone—it will always take as long as it takes—but there are some things you can do to help your heart mend.

Wallow . . . a Little

Years ago, I was unceremoniously dumped by a boyfriend and spent the better part of a day listening to sad music created by other heartbroken people. Allowing myself to shamelessly weep in my cozy bed while wallowing in shared misery was an oddly bittersweet and cathartic experience. But this is a strange pleasure that should be curbed after a day or so.

Connect with Your Friends

When you're going through a breakup, your friends are your best ally. Not only will they love and support you—but they also have a unique perspective. It can be tempting to romanticize a relationship once it's over, but your friends can remind you of all the reasons why you and your ex didn't work out. Seeing your ex through the eyes of the people who love you and know you best can be immensely helpful.

LOVE

Give Yourself a Heartbreak Cleanse

Love can be a little like an addiction—and so the best way to rid yourself of its pull is to completely separate from the source. That means no checking up on your ex on social media, no asking friends what he or she is up to, no pulling out old photos or replaying events over and over again in your head. Instead, when you feel yourself starting to be drawn toward your ex, take a deep breath and commit to filling yourself up with other pleasurable things like eating, dancing, laughing, singing, and, perhaps, even masturbating.

Do Stuff You Like

This should always be a priority, but even more so after a breakup. Or how about trying some new things? This will further help you reclaim your life as your own and fill the void you've been left with. Pause and ask yourself: Is there anything you've been wanting to try? Taking a photography class? Joining a book club? New activities will not only make you feel better about yourself but also open you up to meeting new friends with similar interests.

Remember: happy people attract happy people. If you're enjoying yourself, chances are you'll find your pleasure.

Indulge Yourself

For genuine depictions of female pleasure, check out ethical porn from content creators like Erika Lust, Shine Louise Houston, and Cindy Gallop.

HEAT THINGS UP

When I first started dating Jason, it became clear that we were different kinds of people. Nowhere was this more obvious than in the kitchen. When it came to cooking, I was cautious and tentative, clinging tightly to well-known recipes and reliable measuring cups. I paired that wariness with a creative haphazardness that left the kitchen looking like a poltergeist had recently visited. He actually began to lovingly refer to me as an anarchist in the kitchen.

Jason, on the other hand, was fearless, making dishes up on the fly based on the contents of the fridge. His fearlessness was matched with a meticulous attention to detail. He once decided to make a thatched "hut" out of beans for my girlfriend's birthday because he felt it would be appropriately fancy.

Despite our radically different approaches, we still managed to create a lot of heat between us.

I've since realized that no matter what your style is, there are many things to be learned about pleasure and play when it comes to making meals with or for your partner.

Imagine if we approached our meals the way we approach planning a date with our lovers? Every item we choose, like the sexy items we might wear under our clothes, could aim to provoke or titillate or weave an intoxicating spell. To awaken sleepy taste buds on our palates. To stoke the flames of desire into a frenzied sizzle.

I'm not saying that every meal we have with our partners needs to be drenched in desire. But I think that when we infuse love into our cooking, we magically invoke in our lovers a subtle yet constant craving to continually return to us.

FIND YOUR PLEASURE

LOVE LANGUAGES

Ever have an argument with your partner and think to yourself, *Wow—it's like we're speaking completely different languages?* According to longtime relationship counselor Gary Chapman, there are five different ways, or languages, that you use to show you love someone, and figuring out what your and your partner's top two languages are can improve communication and deepen the connection you have with each other.

Words of Affirmation

If you desire kind, encouraging, and positive words from your partner, this is likely your love language. Hearing "I love you" is nice, of course, but you would rather hear the thoughtful reasons behind your partner's love.

Acts of Service

For some people, actions speak louder than words. These gestures can be as big as your partner taking your car for a tune-up or as simple as bringing you a cup of coffee in the morning. If this is your love language, anything your partner does to lighten your load speaks volumes about their love for you.

Quality Time

Quality doesn't necessarily mean quantity. The key to this love language is your partner spending meaningful time with you, whether that's through sincere conversations or shared activities. Having their undivided attention makes you feel truly loved.

Physical Touch

Physical touch is not just about getting it on in the bedroom—it's about reveling in the slightest contact. With this love language, when your partner gives you a hug, holds your hand, or gently touches your arm, you feel a sense of security and belonging.

Receiving Gifts

Whoever coined the phrase "Diamonds are a girl's best friend" definitely had this as their love language, and it might be yours if even small, unexpected gifts mean more to you than words and actions.

You probably saw yourself in at least two of those descriptions, but what about your partner? Think of how they try to love you. Is it through touch or gifts? What do they ask of you most often? Is it help around the house, or more physical intimacy? What do they say frustrates them the most about your relationship? The answers to those questions will tell you their love languages. Once you both recognize how the other loves and wants to be loved, you'll find pleasure in each gesture.

Pleasure can be seen as something indulgent. Something that's reserved for only a select few and not accessible for all. But everyone—regardless of age, gender identity, cultural background, economic or ability status—deserves to have access to all kinds of pleasures, including intimate ones.

Therapist and author Tuppy Owens agrees. Back in the 1980s she started a UK-based peer-support group, called Outsiders, specifically for those with physical and/or social disabilities. The idea was to bring connection and pleasure to some of the most vulnerable, marginalized, and often touch-starved in society.

This volunteer-run club not only has an online dating site, they also regularly organize events to bring people together who otherwise might never meet. At these events, they even sometimes bring out massage therapists and sex workers to encourage consensual play through all kinds of touch.

So if you've been feeling isolated or alone, consider starting your own "pleasure" group to reach out to those who need intimate connection the most.

Indulge Yourself

Wrap yourself in a warm towel right out of the dryer and sink into relaxation.

H ave you ever been at a restaurant and watched a couple who are sitting through a meal with nothing to say to each other? I find this so disheartening. I'm so grateful to say that after many, many years, I still don't feel as though I know everything about Jason. I don't think that's because we're so special—I think that if we all tapped into our curiosity we could find things to talk to our partner about until the end of time.

Communication is so integral to any relationship, and some experts say that a weekly focused conversation—even a short one—can be the single most important thing a couple can do for their relationship.

So what could that look like? Here's a conversation breakdown to get you started.

Begin with what makes you really happy right now. These don't have to be huge: you can tell your partner you're grateful that he cleaned out the air filters or that she took care of bedtimes this week. Anything that acknowledges often thankless but necessary jobs can do wonders for dissolving potential resentments—and act as a springboard into a practical conversation about what needs tweaking in terms of upcoming chores.

Leave space for both of you to bring up any problems or challenges you're experiencing. Make sure to focus on using "I feel" statements as opposed to "You always . . ." so this isn't framed as an attack. Try to listen without getting defensive. Remember, curiosity is key.

Finish with more pleasurable stuff by scheduling spicy date nights as well as family-fun adventures to look forward to.

One final suggestion: have this conversation in a comfortable and intimate spot like a cozy restaurant or in bed so it doesn't feel like you're having a work meeting.

P.S.: Now you'll never be that quiet couple in the restaurant again!

Pleasure Project

Keep a jar in a well-used room in your house for family members or guests to write down pleasant memories and heartfelt compliments. Whenever someone is having a bad day, they can pull a note from the jar to read for some much-needed pleasure.

LOVE

FIND YOUR PLEASURE

ARGUE BETTER

I've often said that in my relationship, I'm the firecracker and Jason is the molasses. In other words—I am dazzling (ha!), quick, and explosive, whereas he is sweet, slow, and sometimes sticky. Turns out, this kind of relationship dynamic is quite common. Many therapists believe that, in most couples, there is a hailstorm and a turtle and these characteristics become more apparent when a conflict arises. If you're the turtle (or molasses), you turn inward and need alone time to process. If you're the hailstorm (or firecracker), you tend to process the situation outwardly. The more a hailstorm hails, the deeper a turtle withdraws into its shell, and vice versa.

If you want to argue better, it helps to take cues from each other. So turtles need to learn how to push their energy out and express themselves clearly, and hailstorms need to learn to step back and contain their energy.

When you successfully channel some of the uniqueness of your partner, you have a much better chance of hearing each other and getting back on your paths to pleasure sooner.

Indulge Yourself

Lie down naked with a lover or by yourself between warm, freshly washed sheets.

REMEMBER THE
GOOD TIMES

When you're in a relationship that's lasted for years, it's sometimes easy to forget all the good things you once saw in your partner. So here's something you can try: sit down with your partner and share the things that made you fall in love with each other. For noncommunicative couples, this might be the first time you've heard your partner talk out loud about these qualities. As you recall shared memories, any resentments you might harbor will recede to the background and you'll stir up old passionate feelings.

Pleasure Project

For five days, write down one thing each day that your significant other does that you appreciate—even small things like hugs. At the end of the week, give your partner the notes in a creative way (like my mom did for me; see Love Letters, on page 15)—you might find that it inspires him or her to do the same for you!

FIND YOUR PLEASURE

TAKE A VACATION

Studies say that couples experience a sexual "afterglow" up to forty-eight hours after having sex. It turns out that traveling together has even longer-lasting effects. Many couples say that they felt closer to their partners for three to four weeks after their travels. Some say they never lost that travel afterglow!

If you feel your relationship needs a reboot, look at retreats that include couples therapy. They're designed to help couples work through issues, so you will undoubtedly get more, well, bang for your buck. (Yes, I meant to do that!)

Indulge Yourself

Go into an ice cream or candy shop and choose something you've never tried before.

LOVE CHALLENGES

I've read that couples in long-term relationships who try new things report more feelings of passionate love than those who don't. That inspired me to find love challenges for my partner and me. Here are some you can have fun with.

Send Each Other Compliments

When you're in a new relationship, you often overflow with compliments. I remember a note my partner sent that described me as having "sweet skin." But as the years go by, you're less inclined to do this. So try texting each other easy compliments, and then get more specific and honest. We started with things like "I think you're pretty," then moved on to "I am in awe of your skill as a parent."

Get It On in a New Place

Comfortable sex is one of the great advantages of a long-term relationship, but we crave new experiences. Whether it's in a new room in the house or with a new toy, let your imagination go wild.

Go Out and Show Off

Public displays of affection are a great way to re-create the spirit of your early dating days—even something as tame as holding hands. Or find a private space in public and get frisky.

Pull Out Old Pictures

When you revisit memories and recall different aspects of your relationship, it can actually feel like you're recapturing those experiences together.

Make a Playlist for Each Other

Do certain songs evoke the days when you first fell in love? One album in particular reminds me of my first dates with Jason. He took me to a salsa club, and when I hear that music now, I melt. Choose songs that bring back your feelings for each other in the same way.

Sex

FIND YOUR PLEASURE

MAKE YOUR SEX LIFE WORK

Your sexual life will likely ebb and flow throughout your relationship, so instead of trying to "keep up with the Joneses" by putting in some magical number of sex sessions per week or month, focus on quality, not quantity.

Consider expanding what being intimate means for you—in other words, what makes you feel deeply connected to your partner. Maybe it's cuddling, maybe it's a massage, maybe it's taking a shower together. Whatever it is, make pleasure your priority.

Pleasure Prompt

Buy or make a "tickle trunk" and fill it with your favorite erotic items—costumes, games, sensual oils, and adult toys. Lock it up and wear the key around your neck, or keep it in your pleasure pouch (see The Pleasure Within, page 163).

THE PLEASURE GAP

There is the notion that men need sex in different ways than women, and that in order to avoid men straying, women must be as sexually exciting as possible. With such a myth, it's no surprise that there's a pleasure gap between the genders, especially in straight relationships: women are four times more likely to refer to sex as less pleasurable than men. It's not that women are biologically less capable of orgasm—we generally have no problem experiencing orgasm through masturbation—but women who frequently have orgasms during masturbation report many fewer orgasms with a partner. Is this partially because we're focusing on our partners' enjoyment instead of our own?

How can you stop perpetuating myths and close the pleasure gap? Here are some ideas.

Get to Know Yourself

For many women, the urge to have sex doesn't hit quite the way it does for men. Often, especially as you age, desire is born out of action: you get in the mood when you start thinking sexy thoughts or exploring your body. The vagina is great, but not necessarily the place that provides the most pleasure. That's the vulva (which includes your pleasure powerhouse: the clitoris)—say it loud and proud! Cultivating your erotic side helps you focus on your own pleasure rather than the need to "service" your partner. When that happens, both parties benefit.

Let's Talk About Sex!

You need to be open about your desires if you're to find meaningful sexual pleasure. Communication is key, not only with your partner but also when you're teaching your children about sex. We often shame girls for touching themselves but say things like, "Boys will be boys." We also discourage both genders from using the word *vulva* (an umbrella term that includes the clitoris), choosing instead to focus on the word *vagina* (which, for most women, is not at all the place where the most pleasure is derived). When we do that, what we're really saying is that girls' sexuality and pleasure is something to be buried or set aside, but that's simply not true.

Be open about your desires.

Toys, Toys, Toys

According to studies, many women use vibrators and those same women report easier arousal, greater sexual desire, and equal or better sexual satisfaction than women who don't. In other words, sex toys are a great way for women to reclaim pleasure with or without their partner, especially when women feel their bodies are being hijacked by aging or illness or are having trouble becoming aroused.

Honesty Is the Best Policy

There are many reasons to have sex: because you want to feel sensual; give yourself and your partner pleasure; have an orgasm; reconnect. Obligation, however, is a bad reason. Obligatory sex creates resentment and perpetuates a myth about your sexuality to your partner that can't be sustained. Your sex life will undoubtedly change throughout the ups and downs of life. The more honest you are about your desires, and the more you tap into your own pleasures, the more intimate and rewarding your sexual partnerships will be.

Pleasure Project

With ongoing and enthusiastic consent, take turns wearing blindfolds. Play hot/cold, touching the blindfolded person using different items with different textures and temperatures. If the blindfolded person says *cold*, that's a signal to try something else; *hot* means keep going.

TICKET TO PLEASURE

If you're one of those people who hears the word *mindfulness* and rolls your eyes, consider this: research has shown that mindfulness can help break negative thought patterns, reduce stress and anxiety, and sharpen your focus.

All good, right?

Let's face it, we live in a world where our attention is constantly pulled in a million directions. We are overstretched, overstimulated, and overanxious. This tendency toward multitasking affects every part of our lives, including our sex lives. While there are many reasons for low desire, one of them is that we're often on autopilot. In order to have great sex, your brain has to connect to your body, and mindfulness sessions can go a long way to helping with that. Research has also shown that mindfulness can be helpful for women with a wide range of sexual issues—from past trauma and pain to low desire.

Don't get me wrong, I think being on autopilot sometimes during life is great. I'm never going to be mindful doing the dishes—I'm fine singing along to Prince and imagining he's singing just to me. And who hasn't fantasized that they're having sex not with their partner in their bedroom, but in a magical land getting it on with the king and all of his court? (Or is that just me?)

The point is: if you're doing all this fantasizing and it's still not giving you what you want in the bedroom, mindfulness might be your ticket to pleasure.

FIND YOUR PLEASURE

If you want to be in the mood for sex, you sometimes have to go part of the way yourself. As unsexy as it may sound, make a plan to have sex with your partner. We put so much effort into organizing activities with friends and family, it's important to remember to make time for yourself and the person you're most intimate with.

Before you have sex, get in the right headspace by having a bath alone, reading a sexy book, or browsing your favorite erotica site. Breathe. Think about what your body is doing. Maybe put on something you find sexy or spend a few moments with your favorite toy. Before you know it, you'll be revving your engines.

Indulge Yourself

Recall a moment that made your insides melt and inspires you to feel incredibly sexy.

FIND YOUR PLEASURE

So much of our world focuses on how to be sexually appealing to someone else, not on finding pleasure within. But if you're worried about how you look instead of how you feel, your pleasure is instantly compromised. That's why it's so important to train your mind to let go.

Try doing a body scan. Close your eyes, breathe deeply, and begin at your toes. Slide your mind slowly all the way up your body, becoming aware of how each part of your body feels. Pay attention to the subtlest of sensations. Does one area feel hot or cool? Tight or sore? Tingly? Breathe into those areas for five minutes.

Next, try squeezing every part of your body. Your calves, legs, buttocks, hands, arms, chest, shoulders, face, and then . . . release. Notice how your body feels afterward.

Doing this repeatedly brings unique sensations to your body that you don't often experience.

Pleasure Project

Make a pleasure pouch. Repurpose velvet from a vintage dress or lace from an old negligee—
a simple stitch on three sides will do the trick. Or use a dazzling purse you've retired. Then, fill it
with items that bring you great pleasure—essential oils, soft fabric that feels sensual and/or holds
memories, photographs, love letters. Add notes about your dreams, favorite mottos, and more.
Check in on this pouch whenever you need a hit of pleasure.

A TURN TO THE EROTIC

L et's face it, we all have unsexy things vying for our attention. Dirty laundry and unwashed dishes, unscheduled appointments, stressful Twitter feeds—I could go on and on. So is it any wonder that at the end of the day so many of us say, "I'm not in the mood"?

One of the simplest ways to let go of anxiety and tap into your fantasy life is to use erotic stories. It can be amazing what a sexy story in your brain can do for your body in the sheets—whether it's a memory of a sexy romp from your past, or actually diving into a risqué novel involving characters engaging in things you'd never try in your real life.

If you don't know where to start when it comes to written erotica, I suggest you check out the work of the late Nancy Friday. She published several collections of real women's sexual fantasies in the seventies and eighties, and these books are a candid reminder that the things that bring women pleasure are as diverse and varied as women themselves.

When your imagination is creatively primed with erotic stories that you can tap into at any time, chances are you'll more easily find pleasure in your real-life sexual experiences.

Indulge Yourself

Turn off the lights and breathe deeply. Clear your mind of distractions, and let your imagination loose.

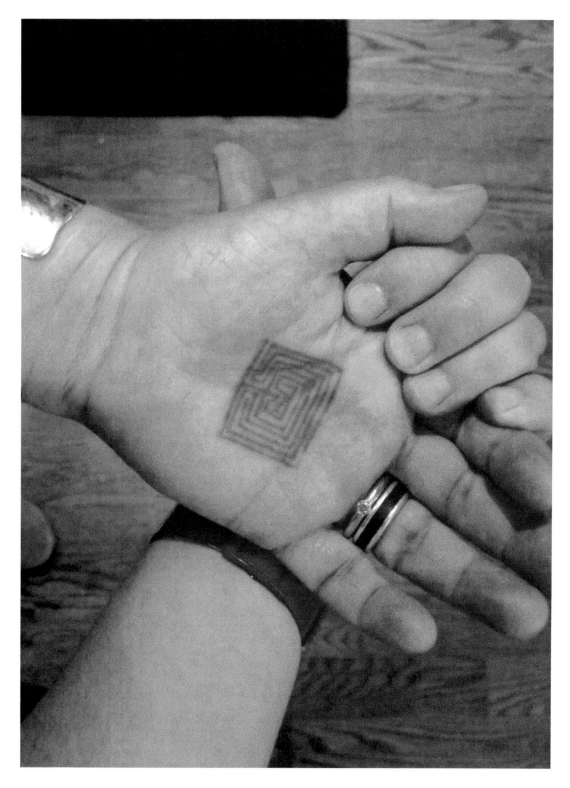

FIND YOUR PLEASURE

THE KEY TO "CASUAL" SEX

First of all, I'm not sure sex can be *casual*. Sex (in its myriad forms) is big, loud, heady, and messy. When you have sex, your oxytocin levels increase, which promotes bonding with others. By its very *nature*, sex is not casual.

And semantics aside, studies show that while women often regret their casual sexual encounters, high-quality sex rarely leads to remorse. The more enjoyable the sex, the less the regret. What makes sex enjoyable? Many things, including good conversation, feeling safe, and mutual pleasure. In other words, you need to have some amount of care and concern for the other person to experience good sex.

So now I'm back to semantics. Instead of looking at sex as *casual*, what if we viewed it as significant and pleasure-filled? Noncommittal? Great! Hot hookup? Terrific! Whatever makes it both sound and be delicious and respectful. Then maybe we can have more pleasure and less regret.

TOUCH EACH OTHER

It's easy to fall into ruts over time. Maybe you always eat at the same restaurants, hang out with the same friends, sleep in the same positions. Then one day you wake up and realize you've both been sleepwalking through your relationship.

Sometimes the best way to rev things up is to delay things.

That's where sensate focus comes in. Originally conceived by marital therapists William H. Masters and Virginia E. Johnson of Masters and Johnson fame, it's mindfulness exercises designed for couples who want to reconnect. They're usually done with the remote guidance of a sex therapist, but anyone can benefit from the general principles. Instead of a baseball approach to sex, sensate focus isn't goal-oriented—it's about nondemand touching. The idea is to get out of your head, into your body, and enjoy touch for the sheer pleasure. Here are some ideas you can try.

Sit or lie down naked together. You may want to have soft fabrics, scented candles, or gentle music on hand to enhance your pleasure.

Take turns being toucher and receiver; you'll switch roles after about thirty minutes.

The toucher may explore their partner's body everywhere but the genitals and experiment with different kinds of touches, from soft and fluttery to firm and intense. Notice the pleasure in feeling all the different textures—soft, bumpy, furry—your lover has.

The receiver breathes deeply and focuses on the sensations of being touched. If your mind wanders or says negative things, push those thoughts aside and bring your focus back to what you're feeling physically.

Gently redirect by saying things like "too tickly" or "too firm" if you're being touched in a way that feels uncomfortable. And when your lover gets the touch just right, be sure to tell him or her so.

If you get aroused during this process, it's fine, it's just not the goal.

Eventually, you may incorporate genital touching, and, when you're both ready, intercourse.

There are so many benefits to slowing down, savoring, and simplifying the process of touch. You may find that focusing on these simple sensations unlocks pleasure pockets you didn't even know you had. Ultimately sensate focus should allow you to release expectations and simply "be" with your body and your partner's in the moment. In this way, it takes the emphasis off "performance" goals and expectation and is a reminder that in the vast buffet of pleasure intercourse is simply one dish.

Pleasure Project

Want to have more and better orgasms? Squeeze the same muscles that you would use to stop the flow of pee, hold for five seconds, and relax. Build from there. Several products can help with these exercises—aka Kegels—and also double as erotic toys.

CHANGE YOUR POSITION

While it might not be the goal for everyone all the time, orgasm is, by definition, peak pleasure. But not all positions are going to put your pleasure train on the right track. If you're concentrating on maintaining a circus-like contortion so that you don't crack your head or wondering what your body looks like in a pretzeled position, chances are you're not focusing on what your genitals are feeling.

Certain positions simply work better for bodies with vulvas. Like the CAT, which is a great name for obvious reasons but stands for coital alignment technique (also somewhat hilariously known as grinding the corn). It's a subtle but important variation on the missionary position that maximizes clitoral stimulation. His or her pelvis starts out a bit lower than yours and then rocks forward as you tilt your pelvis upward until your pelvises align.

Many women also report having orgasms during intercourse when they're on top because it's easy to control movement, so think of moving your hips in circles, figure eights, and back and forth, all of which will stimulate your clitoris. If you tend to masturbate on your stomach, you may find that intercourse from behind works well. Or perhaps on your side because you can use your hands—perhaps to hold tools to aid in the process.

The only way to find out is to try, try, and try again!

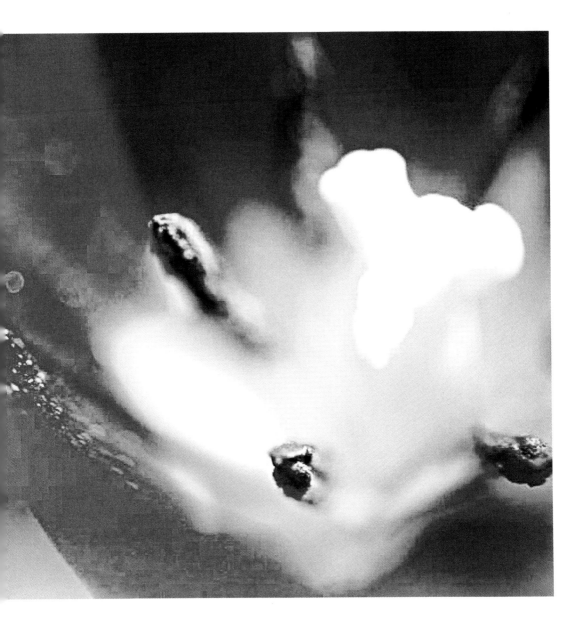

LOVE

FIND YOUR PLEASURE

SEX AND PARENTING

Just had a baby? Congratulations! You're likely beginning to realize that parenting is one hell of a roller-coaster ride. Now picture attempting sex on that roller coaster. Laughable, right? And by laughable I mean challenging, awkward, and more than a little scary. So how do you delight in your adorable new addition without completely forsaking your mojo? Here are some ideas.

Give Yourself a Break

You've just had your vagina stretched to the size of a butternut squash or you've been sliced open like a ripe watermelon. Naturally, it's completely normal if you aren't interested in having anything else poking around down there. Depending on how your labor went, how much sleep you're getting, and how connected you feel to your partner, the process of getting back into sex may take anywhere from a month to . . . what year am I in now?

Explore New Sensations

If you're in the mood but still unsure about intercourse, consider taking that option off the table (what are you doing having sex on the table anyway—ha!). Instead, commit to creating space for other kinds of intimacy to unfold, which will take the pressure off both of you.

Make a Date "Moment"

If an entire date night feels too ambitious, try for a moment. Carve out twenty minutes to have a glass of wine or shower together. Or cuddle and just sleep. Whatever you do, make sure remember that mutual pleasure and connection is your only goal.

MAP OUT YOUR JOURNEY

One of the most common sexual complaints I hear about is low desire, particularly from women. So much emphasis is placed on desire, but isn't whether you experience pleasure more important? Here are some ideas on how to stoke your own fires.

Lose the Brakes

In her book *Come as You Are*, Emily Nagoski compares our brains to cars. We have a sexual "accelerator" that responds to all the stuff we find sexy, like risqué pictures of people we find attractive. (A shirtless Jason Momoa for me? Yep.) But we also have sexual "brakes"—distractions that can be as simple as your toddler calling out or as complicated as feeling like you don't fully trust your partner. Getting in the mood requires us to turn on our ONs and turn off our OFFs. It's a conscious exercise, but well worth the effort.

Hit the Gas

Most women experience desire a little differently than men. We don't necessarily spontaneously feel aroused—it's more likely that we *respond* to sexual situations. In other words, once we're in a sexual situation with touching and kissing, *then* our desire for sex grows. So if you're still not in the mood, ladies, give yourself a break, especially if you're in a long-term monogamous relationship and/or you have little unpredictable freeloaders (I'm talking about kids) waking up and demanding shit (or having shits) at all hours. All that can take the focus off erotic desire, but the good news is that it's easy to get back into the groove.

Pleasure Prompt

Lube is your friend always, but especially postpartum and postmenopausal. There are ones that glide, tingle, warm, or taste good. Find the one that is safest and most pleasurable for you, whether water-, oil-, or silicone-based.

Inspire

Creativity

HIDDEN MESSAGES

Years ago, I had the good fortune to sit down with *Eat, Pray, Love* author Elizabeth Gilbert on *The Social*. Her presence was felt as soon as she entered our backstage area. Effortlessly beautiful, dressed in a sharp yet casual suit, she had a calm, grounded energy that radiated around her in the most amazing way.

She was on our show to talk about her book *Big Magic*, which is all about embracing curiosity and tapping into your creative potential. One of the ideas she writes about is that there are a finite number of creative ideas in the world, and if you don't grab a hold of one of yours when it comes knocking, it will simply move along and find another person who is ready to receive it.

As Elizabeth was speaking, I couldn't help but feel that she was communicating directly to me—after all, I'd had a dream of launching a website but hadn't yet gotten it off the ground. Her words were just the push I needed. After the interview was done, we went backstage, and she opened up a cloth bag and asked everyone to reach in and pull something out. I unearthed a small charm of the elephant god, Ganesh. Elizabeth smiled at me in a kind of knowing way, we embraced, and then she was gone.

Right away, I did whatever any magical-thinking person would: I began researching the meaning behind this talisman. Seems Ganesh (also Ganesa or Ganesha) is the lord of good fortune and new beginnings. He's often seen as a remover of obstacles, both the material and spiritual variety, and he also sometimes places obstacles in the paths of those who need to be checked. Ahem.

I was recently reminded of that when I got home from work one day feeling incredibly anxious. You know that tight-chested, cold, sweaty feeling, as if a cloud of doom is hanging over you?

After dinner my son said, "Mommy, I need you to help me make a dragon."

I thought, *I don't know how to make a fucking dragon.*

But I unearthed a cardboard box, and we started. We cut construction paper into triangles. Added colorful spots. Decorated with sparkly tape. And, voilà, a dragon! After he wore it around on his head for a while, he said, "Mommy, this is your dragon."

That felt like both a sweet and significant gesture, so after he went to bed, I looked up the meaning of dragons. It seems they are believed to be powerful guardians and guides, and are there for those who need strength, courage, and fortitude.

Suddenly I noticed that all my anxiety was gone.

The universe is constantly sending messages. When you tune in and truly listen, these messages can help you liberate secret parts of yourself and let your creative spirit soar. And that's some kind of big magic indeed.

FIND YOUR FLOW

I was on my first 10k run. I was acutely aware of my body. I was sweaty; I was tired; I had a stitch. But then—out of nowhere—it was as if I had opened a door into another dimension. I was hovering above myself, completely detached. A sense of calm and clarity washed over me, and I felt like I was being pulled forward, drawn toward a state of ecstatic pleasure.

After I was done, all I could think was *Sign me up for that feeling again!*

I now know that experience has a name. It's called "flow."

Flow is brought on by meaningful work—physical or mental—and has been described as a feeling of deep connection and fulfillment. But many believe it's a state of consciousness, the most productive and creative state of mind, and that achieving flow regularly is a key component of happiness. That makes sense: when you think about it, our bodies are primed for flow—blood and water are constantly moving within us.

Here are tips on how to access the pleasure of flow.

Think about what you'd do if money was no object and you had plenty of time. It doesn't matter what—writing a screenplay, decorating, or gardening.

Find what's "just right." If something is too easy, your mind may wander. If it's too hard, you risk feeling overwhelmed.

Set goals and break big tasks into smaller bits—write your novel for fifteen minutes a day, get out and train for that marathon three times a week for thirty minutes, or work in your garden every morning for an hour.

Tune out distractions: turn off notifications, use apps that block you from internet searches or social media, or put your phone away completely.

Set a timer—at least fifteen minutes are needed to get into the flow state.

Rev yourself up! Jog around the block, dance around the room, or watch or read something that inspires you.

Seek out calming things if you're anxious, angry, or distracted. Go for a walk and breathe deeply, listen to a meditation app, make tea, or take a shower.

Then begin again.

FIND YOUR PLEASURE

LEARN TO PLORK

You may not consider yourself an artist, or even an art connoisseur. But I'll bet you're already aware, dear reader, that art is an essential part of pleasure. Imagine for a moment a world where there are no paintings, no sculptures, no movies, no graphic design, no music. That would be a world with no pleasure.

Corita Kent intensely recognized the power and purpose of art. She was a pop artist, social activist, and teacher. She also happened to be a nun. While teaching art at Immaculate Heart College in California, she created a unique set of rules for her class. They included the following:

- Find a place you trust and then try trusting it for a while.

- Nothing is a mistake. There is no win and no fail. There is only make.

- Be happy whenever you can manage it. Enjoy yourself. It's lighter than you think.

Sister Corita understood that in order to create art, we need to remove obstacles that block our inner artists and learn to see things differently. One of the ways she suggested we do that is to observe the way children navigate a familiar space. If you've ever done that, you quickly realize that for small children especially, every day is a journey filled with touching, smelling, tasting, and shaking. Basically, kids tap into their creativity and vitality through pleasure.

Sister Corita also suggested that people make time for "plorking"—a clever word combining *play* and *work*. Whether this means getting up and taking a walk, reading a book, or seeing a movie, the idea is that the process of play is as necessary and important as work.

So doodle, dance, wander, and plork, and unleash your inner virtuoso.

Pleasure Project

Grab a paintbrush and splash some paint on a piece of paper.
Tuck it in a frame when it's dry.

THE PLEASURE OF MENTORING

Former US secretary of state Madeleine Albright once said, "There is a special place in hell for women who don't help other women." I'm not sure we can say that's an absolute truth, but I do think there is something important about supporting other women.

When I was starting in television, there were women I would have loved to get guidance from. But at best, I found them distant and intimidating; at worst, mean and ostracizing. I don't totally blame them. For a long time it felt like women in this industry were playing an awful game of musical chairs—once you got one of the coveted seats at the table, you sure as hell weren't going to get up. Thankfully, as women have fought for and won more seats, there's more mentoring, which is infinitely more pleasurable for everyone.

I've been lucky since then to have those who saw something in me that I didn't even necessarily see in myself, and who pushed and nurtured me. In turn, I've had the opportunity to share my experiences with younger people, and have found there's a real sense of accomplishment when I witness their successes.

Reverse mentoring is also becoming popular, as businesses acknowledge that younger people climbing the corporate ladder have things to teach those who have been around longer—their fresh, unencumbered way of thinking means they often come up with imaginative ideas.

When you help others, something magical happens, and we expand our humanity.

FIND YOUR PLEASURE

SEIZE THE DAY

Are you sitting on the sidelines of life or are you in the game? For years, my instinct was to sit and watch—it felt safer. But then I started to notice all the people around me who were fearless about diving in.

I was on vacation once and saw someone stand-up paddleboarding. My first thought was *Wow, that looks cool—I could never do that.* Then I was like: *Fuck that. Sure I can!* The experience was thrilling—like walking on water—the sublime joy of being suspended over the water mixed with a little bit of nervousness about crashing and falling, but the experience was exhilarating.

Since then, I've tried snorkeling, boogie boarding, and even had a very embarrassing but thrilling karaoke experience in front of a room full of strangers.

Is there an area in your life where you've held back? You might find an unexpected pleasure if you try seizing the day!

FIND YOUR PLEASURE

BALANCE IN LIFE

A mbition can be a pleasure sucker. Have you ever chased a dream only to realize that, instead of filling your days with things you love, your time goes to endless obligations? I'll admit, there were times when I was writing this book that I realized I hovered on the brink of burnout (which is ironic given that my whole philosophy is to make life more pleasurable, not more painful). Unless you genuinely derive pleasure from the stresses and pressures of the idea of "success," chances are you might need to balance productivity with pleasure.

Here are things I've learned along the way that will help you to do just that.

Say No

It's okay to cancel plans or to pass on a new assignment. Will you miss a few opportunities? Yes. But will there be other ones (perhaps, better ones) around the corner? Yes! In the long run, you'll benefit more from setting the right habits and being productive consistently than overworking yourself to the point where you end up flaming out before your light truly gets to shine.

Schedule Offline Downtime

It's far too easy nowadays to spend "breaks" mindlessly scrolling through our phones seeking out quick hits of pleasure that do nothing but numb our minds or emotions. So go for a walk. Grab a coffee. Truly reset. Then go back to work. Trust me, you'll find you're more productive.

Assess Goals

There's more to success than moving up in the work world. If your aim is to retire at sixty-five and travel the world, maybe working extra hours and sacrificing some pleasures now is worth it. But if your goal is to spend more time with your kids, reconsider how many hours you're putting in at the office. At the end of the day, only you can define what success means for you.

THE POWER OF JOURNALING

When I was in my early twenties, I was reading *The Artist's Way* by Julia Cameron and began writing three pages of stream-of-consciousness thoughts every morning—she recommended this as a way to tap into and unleash your inner artist. When I went back and read what I had written, it was revelatory.

At the same time, I was a smoker and was convinced it was a huge pleasure in my life. But my journal showed me that every morning, while in a half-asleep state, my first waking thought was *I have to quit smoking*. It was an honest, vulnerable truth that I conveniently pushed aside as soon as I had my morning coffee. Reading that allowed me to recognize how this supposed pleasure was causing me pain. If I'd never begun journaling, I wonder if or when I would have been able to hear that inner voice.

Here are some ideas on how to create your own journal and perhaps find your own truths.

Choose a book that speaks to you—big or small, blank or lined pages, with or without dates, maybe even with a lock and key.

Journal in a style that brings you pleasure: as simple as writing down a few lines about your day, with drawings using fancy, colorful markers, or with stickers. There are no rules. If you search online for *bullet journals*, you'll find endless inspirations.

Aim to get into a flow state when you're writing. Cameron suggests writing a set number of pages or for a set amount of time (for instance, three pages or for three minutes straight) without taking your pen off the page. Even if you only write *I can't think of anything to write*, eventually something will come through.

Whether you write bullet-pointed words that describe your emotions throughout your day, add captions to photographs, or document how you feel about what comes out of your child's mouth—it's all part of your ever-evolving story.

FIND YOUR PLEASURE

PLEASURABLE WORKDAYS

If you're arriving at work every Monday under a shadow of dread, something has to change. We spend at least a third of our lifetimes at work, so ideally our jobs will be fulfilling. But if your current job is just a stepping-stone to achieving a bigger dream, there are going to be days when you want to throw in the towel, sponge, or any other absorbent material you can find. Even if you love your job, you still might have these days.

The good news is that you can carve out small spaces in your day and actively pour pleasure into them.

Do One Thing Differently

It's simple: eat at a different restaurant for lunch, spend your break calling someone you haven't spoken to in a while, sleep in once a week. Scheduling nuggets of unexpected delight gives you something to look forward to.

Surround Yourself with Joyful Things

Fill your workspace with things that delight your senses—a pick-me-up song playlist, photos of loved ones, emergency candies, deliciously scented lotion, or essential oils to banish stress and headaches.

Work Smarter, Not Harder

If your current job is a way to pay the bills, approach it with commitment and proficiency but save your ambition, imagination, and creativity for personal endeavors and grab five or ten minutes when you can to focus on what matters most to you.

Spread the Love

Every morning, Benjamin Franklin would ask himself, "What good will I do today?" and just before bed, "What good have I done today?" You, too, have the ability to make a positive impact, whether it's giving someone a smile or asking about their day.

BIG BANG

The BIG O

LOU PAGET

groneman

nymphomania

1000 Dessous

Gilles Néret

THE OTHER WORLDS
OF BOOKS

My love of reading was first inspired by my mother and further solidified via a teacher who would weave the most vivid stories: tales of misunderstood monsters, powerful princesses, and fantastical follies. Since then, one of my greatest pleasures in life is reading.

I am clearly not alone. We are wired for storytelling. We crave archetypal tales. For countless generations, this is how cultures around the world have shared wisdom and kept the memories of ancestors alive. Stories allow us access into the worlds of our imaginations and our dreams—worlds we long to be a part of or are very thankful we are not.

I still get a surge of excitement whenever I walk into a library or bookstore. That unique smell and the sight of shelves filled with the contents of someone's imagination are among the most magical joys we have in life. Every night before bed, I feel this pull to revisit the characters of whatever story I'm reading. They've become my friends—I can't help but miss them when they're gone.

Reading is not only a pleasure—it also has a purpose. Research shows that it can reduce stress more than other methods of relaxation. Six minutes are all you need to slow your heart rate down enough to improve your health.

So pick up a book today and escape, into another world and into health and pleasure.

MINDFULNESS

One day I was driving my son to school and decided to stop for a much-needed coffee for me and a buttery croissant for him. I paid the barista, rushed back to the car, tucked my son into his car seat, drove off—and watched my coffee fly off the roof and explode all over my car. And I was reminded of the importance of being mindful.

Mindfulness is a real buzzword these days. You might ask, "What the heck is it exactly?" It's about tuning into the details around you— being aware of the sights, sounds, smells, and textures surrounding us every moment, every day, instead of being on autopilot.

My coffee fiasco was a perfect example of being on autopilot. That can happen anytime, even during sex—you do a little of this and that, your mind wanders, and suddenly you're planning what to have for dinner tomorrow.

To focus on the here and now, try this exercise: Look around. What is one thing that you can see? Another you can hear? Taste? Feel? Smell? Now try doing that same exercise while you're cooking, showering, cleaning, playing with your children, or having sex (see The Pleasure Within on page 163 for more on that).

Mindfulness not only provides a mental break, it also allows us to experience a deep sense of pleasure in *whatever* we're doing.

FIND YOUR PLEASURE

PREPARE AND PRACTICE

For years I worked quietly, invisibly, behind the scenes as a television producer. But when the bottom fell out of the economy, I was certain my job was in jeopardy. I decided to try on-camera stuff, with the encouragement of my boss. I can't describe to you the abject terror I felt when I first started. I felt sweaty, sick to my stomach, completely incapable of stringing a sentence together. But eventually, those feelings started to dissipate. Why? I enrolled in Toastmasters (an international nonprofit organization in which people learn how to work through their public-speaking fears by regularly speaking in front of strangers—friendly strangers, but strangers nevertheless).

Whether you have to give a presentation at work, become comfortable on television, or just give a toast at a wedding—something like that can do wonders helping you if you're afraid of public speaking. Then I took some performance classes in New York and even joined an improvisation group in Toronto. The more I did, the more I found I learned and the less I feared.

The same applies to almost anything. If you're scared of a job interview, get to know the company inside and out and do some role-playing with someone. If you're scared of driving, take lessons and then go on short trips at first, gradually increasing the distance. My sister was afraid of flying, and she downloaded a flight simulator that she regularly watched in the weeks leading up to a trip—getting all the sights and the sounds of a flight. And it worked! Pretty much any problem related to these types of fears can be solved by practice and preparation, and then you can find the joy in what you're doing.

REVEL IN NAPPING

To me there is nothing more refreshing and indulgent than an afternoon nap. And nod your head if you think there is nothing more delightful than bringing a toddler into bed for a nap. Or how about being on vacation and having a post-sex nap with a lover?

When my son was a newborn, naps were one of the few things keeping me sane. My grandfather had an afternoon nap every single day, and he lived until he was one hundred. Before she left *The Huffington Post*, Arianna Huffington opened two nap rooms there. She would openly nap in her office—that's how strongly she believes in the magical powers of naps. She's not alone. Google, Procter & Gamble, Facebook, and the University of Michigan all provide some kind of sleep zone.

That's not surprising, once you consider the incredible amount of money lost in productivity every year. Studies also increasingly show that teens, in particular, suffer greatly from sleep deprivation, which often leads to depression, anxiety, and, eventually, overmedication. Naps can increase alertness, boost productivity and creativity, lower the risk of disease, and leave people better able to regulate emotions—naps literally make you a better person.

There are brain researchers who believe that not only should employers permit their employees to nap at work, but also that staff should be able to work whichever hours are best suited to their lives. Personally, I can't imagine napping at work along with a bunch of colleagues. I don't want to feel like I'm at preschool, or listen to other people as they sleep. But I'm 100 percent behind the idea of people working whatever hours suit them (if they get their work done). In this world where we are constantly plugged in anyway, I think we can all agree that the eight-hour office day should be put to bed.

In the meantime, indulge in blissful, guilt-free naps whenever possible.

FIND YOUR PLEASURE

Dance is all about surrendering, author Henry Miller once said.

Anyone who has ever watched a child move knows we all start off as natural, uninhibited little movers, right from the womb. Then we grow up, get self-conscious, and no longer surrender.

As a young child I remember leaping across hardwood floors in pale pink slippers and ill-fitting tights. I went on to learn the fine art of jazz hands and once performed in an electric-blue ensemble to the incredibly annoying "We Built This City" by Starship.

As I entered my awkward, body-conscious teenage years, I temporarily abandoned dance. But dance didn't abandon me. As soon as I discovered the Grateful Dead, Led Zeppelin, and psychedelic drugs, I began performing wild improvised routines in the dark holding incense sticks. At twenty-one, a Lebanese woman began teaching me the fine art of belly dance. I spent the next ten years dancing everywhere and anywhere—from hookah-infused bars to sweaty gay clubs to lofty ballrooms to grand theaters.

I loved every aspect of it. And let's be real: I also liked being watched. I wanted my audience to get lost in a trance of juicy hips and flowery flourishes, the way I felt whenever I watched a dancer I loved. There were only a handful of times when I let my narcissism get out of the way long enough for me to experience a kind of out-of-body experience. I felt high, ecstatic, disembodied—as though I was connected to something primal and ancient. Surrendering.

I haven't been dancing lately. And that makes me sad. I think, as humans, we need to dance. Studies show that seniors who dance frequently have a reduced risk of dementia, and also that dancing slows down aging, improves muscle memory, and actually makes you smarter!

So here's my challenge. Go find a song you love. Put it on, loud. Then dance like you don't give a fuck.

Indulge Yourself

Buy a brightly colored umbrella that makes you happy on dark, dull days. Go out and splash in puddles, and dance in the rain.

FIND YOUR PLEASURE

FACE YOUR FEARS

I'm an anxious person. Whenever I'm faced with a new scenario, I tend to get panicky. I've also had several full-blown anxiety attacks. But if there's one thing I learned a long time ago, it's that I have to face my fears in order to get the most pleasure out of life.

When I was around ten years old, I went to a magic show, and the magician asked for volunteers. My hand shot up, and he asked me to join him on the stage. Suddenly my stomach did a flip-flop, and I shook my head. I'd decided it was better to stay with my family rather than risk facing . . . embarrassment? Shame? Abject terror? The charming magician moved on and chose a little blond girl. At the end of his trick he gave her a teddy bear.

I. Was. Devastated.

I didn't recognize it then, but it was a good lesson on how succumbing to fear can kill joy and opportunity. Fear of being hurt can hold you back from love. Concerns about safety can keep you from seeing the world. Fear of being seen as "bossy" can mean you get passed over for leadership positions. You can also simply get stuck doing what feels comfortable. But you never know where you could end up if your ship never leaves the port.

How do you get over your fears to discover the pleasures that await? When you're having negative thoughts—I like to call it "awfulizing"—try replacing those thoughts with more realistic ones. Notice I didn't say "positive thoughts." Let's face it, not every situation in life can be spun into gold, but this can help prevent you from going down a negativity spiral. For instance, I would always call Jason before a dance performance and say, "I don't know why I do this, I hate this feeling." And he'd say, "That nervous energy is just misplaced excitement."

And after the nerves, anxiousness, and fear, sweetness comes on the other side: the pleasure of knowing that you overcame those feelings, shared your voice or talents with others, and faced a challenge head-on.

Instead of being an audience member to your life, choose to be onstage and live life fully.

LET THINGS SIMMER

Cupcakes can teach you many things about pleasure.

The most obvious is that life is too short not to eat cupcakes every now and again. But it's in the process of making them that I have learned something that I want to share with you, dear reader.

My favorite cupcake to bake is chocolate with dark chocolate ganache frosting and salted caramel filling. If you've never made caramel from scratch, let me tell you, it is a tricky business! If you remove the caramel from the burner too early, it ends up a slushy, pale mess (basically just melted sugar). If you wait even seconds too long, it will be hard, burnt, and inedible.

So you have to watch and wait, wait and watch. But when you time it just right, then you have the perfect caramel, in all its thick, buttery, sweet glory.

It's the same when it comes to your life, isn't it?

So many of your best ideas, decisions, and even relationships require the right amount of simmering. You need to be patient. You need to focus on the task at hand. You need to recognize that timing is everything. If you do, the pleasure you will feel will be sublime.

Just like the deliciousness of cupcakes.

Wandering

BE AN EXPLORER

Anyone who has children or pets knows that they maneuver through life differently than the rest of us. They touch, sniff, and occasionally put stuff in their mouth that they shouldn't. They have no care about getting anywhere, no concern about the time.

For so many of us, myself included, it's hard to find a blank day on your calendar. And even if you do find one, chances are you will fill that day with little maintenance things like grocery shopping, tidying the house, cleaning out your in-box, and making more to-do lists. When was the last time you simply wandered?

Right now, you could stop reading this book and wander around your home. Go do it.

Great! How did that feel?

Next time, how about meandering around a garden? A park? A forest? A museum? A gallery? Your lover?

Wherever you choose to wander, your only job is to look, explore, and take in. Where appropriate, you can also listen, smell, taste, and touch. A true wander has no agenda or plan, and when you try to interfere with that, things can, well, go sideways.

Near my house there's a well-worn bike path that I've traveled down countless times. I've noticed little nooks or particular foliage and thought about getting off my bike and exploring, but I never did. One day I slowed down, hopped off my bike, and just stood on the path for a moment.

A voice (you know the one!) started shouting at me from inside my head.

"What are you doing? This is booorring! And kinda scary, too. What if there's a bear or a murderer hiding in the trees?"

But after a few minutes, that voice started to get tired and a calmness came over me.

That's when a deer wandered out in front of me. The two of us locked eyes. It was like there was nothing else in the world except for me and her. All I could hear was the rustling of the trees. We stayed there like that for an unknown amount of time, and then she slowly trotted away.

That was a reminder to me of the beautiful and unexpected treasures that wandering can bring.

FIND YOUR PLEASURE

D o less."

It was a message a friend of mine put on her social media. It stood out because it was so counter to all the other messages I saw.

We live in a fast-food world. We celebrate multitaskers who always rush around. Yet our world of "faster" and "more" creates habits that are neither good for our planet nor lend themselves to pleasure.

This simple instruction to do less reminded me of a time when I traveled to a sleepy town in Spain and ordered a *café con leche* to go. The barista looked at me, asked, "*¿Qué?*" then gave me my coffee in a porcelain mug. At first I was slightly miffed. But as I sat in a rickety chair in that old building and started to take in the sights and the smells and the sounds around me, I realized I would have missed all of that if I'd just walked off with my coffee.

And that planted a seed in my heart, a tiny radical way to embrace pleasure: start getting things *to stay*. Sit and sip your coffee, eat your meal slowly, relish your wine, savor that dessert. Then apply this idea of *slow* to other parts of your life. Try slow parenting. How about slow sex? When you start to slow down—when you embrace doing less—that's when the real pleasures of life start to reveal themselves.

Indulge Yourself

Stay in your pajamas all day. Binge-watch all the shows you love.

THE JOY OF THE JOURNEY

One of the greatest gifts in life is the ability to travel. Besides the rejuvenating feeling of being away from your regular routine and spaces, when you experience new places and cultures—when you smell, eat, touch, and see different things—you better understand the world. But half the pleasure of travel comes from the anticipation of the trip.

When I was in my twenties, I traveled to Egypt with a group of women I danced with, despite the misgivings of our friends and families that it might be dangerous. I'm so thankful we went. Not only did we see some of the oldest and most incredible artifacts on the planet, we also experienced great kindness from strangers. One night we were going to see a late music show and dance performance at a nearby hotel, but the cabdriver was trying to charge too much, so at the last minute we decided to walk. A concierge at our hotel was so nervous about our safety he insisted on accompanying us and refused to take any money.

Of course, sometimes things can go wrong. A few years ago, my dad was pickpocketed when my parents were in Italy, and the next day, he was quite tense about being on a crowded train. My mother, sensing this, went to gently kiss his arm, which was holding on to a strap for support, but when she looked up a few moments later, she realized that the arm she had just kissed belonged to another man! Every time my family remembers this story, we double over in laughter.

Travel is like this. You have good times and bad times, but they end up being part of the story of your life. And what a pleasure it is to revisit those memories.

Pleasure Prompt

Planning a trip can be a lot of work, so don't forget to revel in the anticipation leading up to it. And remember, some of the most pleasurable experiences in life are the ones that aren't totally mapped out.

FIND YOUR PLEASURE

SUMMER VACATION LESSONS

I am a creature of habit. I wake up every day around 7:00 a.m., check email, make coffee, play with my son, go to work, attempt some form of exercise, come home, make dinner, watch TV with my partner, and go to bed. Rinse, repeat. I'm sure you have a similar schedule.

I don't mind this repetitiveness—in fact, there are lots of delightfully unexpected moments. But sometimes, it gets a little, well, predictable.

So on one family vacation, I decided I would try to relinquish control. At first it was hard. I worried about our travel schedule. I worried that throwing my son off his schedule would turn him into a bear. I worried a lot. But we managed!

The best part was waking up with almost no plans. We'd loll about in bed. I would wander around. My son and I would play, and entirely lose track of time. There was even a little romance—which, let's face it, often gets forgotten when you have a busy life.

I also unplugged from the internet, avoiding my normal habit of checking my email upon waking, and soon realized that my brain is at its absolute sharpest first thing in the morning. That meant that every day, I usually was using my best brainpower on work emails and social media. So I made a pact to not check my phone until I've done some writing and spent time with my family.

Give yourself a chance to discover what works best for you by temporarily throwing your schedule out the window. Then assess how you feel when you return to your regularly scheduled life. Perhaps you'll discover a whole new—and better—set of habits.

Pleasure Project

- If you normally get up and exercise, instead have a quiet moment to yourself.

- If you tend to fill up your children's schedule, let them take the lead and plan certain days.

- If you spend weekends cleaning, limit your time doing that—then fill the rest of your weekend with something you *want* to do.

- If you have romantic times in the evenings, try out an afternoon delight.

FIND YOUR PLEASURE

LESSONS FROM CHERRY BLOSSOMS

For those of you who don't live in a four-season climate, cherry blossom trees represent one of the first signs that spring is officially "on." What is extra special about them is that blooming season, while glorious, is very short-lived. After the delicate pink or white flowers open, they almost immediately begin to fall, looking like snow on the ground.

In the city where I live, there is a park filled with hundreds of cherry blossom trees, so people come from far and wide to bask in their glory. I hate crowds, and I also get anxious easily, but, recently, I decided to brave the bustle to honor these precious blossoms.

I packed up my son along with some picnicky things and headed out. I drove across the city, found parking, and then trekked through the enormous park only to discover that the blossoms weren't quite fully open yet. I'll admit I thought, *Maybe I would have been better off just admiring something at a garden center closer to home.* But once we were settled, I couldn't help but feel charmed. The park was packed with others who were all out for the same reason: to acknowledge and celebrate the magic of cherry blossoms.

I quickly realized that this time-honored tradition isn't really about the incredible beauty of the blossoms at all. What people are drawn to is the fact that these flowers are a reminder of the fragile impermanence of life. It's not surprising that they are hugely popular in Japan—they are a potent metaphor for Buddhist themes like mortality, mindfulness, and living in the present.

You can't predict when anything will change; all you can do is try your best to celebrate little moments as if they, like the cherry blossoms, might at any second blow away in the wind.

Pleasure
Prompt

Find a kite of a bird or a butterfly, something that represents your inner power animal. Then watch it soar and imagine yourself up there with it.

FIND YOUR PLEASURE

LIFE IS A HIGHWAY

Cars are emblematic of a kind of freedom, aren't they? Most of us can relate to that first exhilarating experience of driving alone when we were teens. For me, it was in my parents' white 1980s Buick with a baby-blue velour interior. Nowadays, though, I have to work to find pleasure in my commute. I'm sure you can relate. Here are some of the things I use to get back that sense of joy I once found in driving.

Listen to Something

Whether it's your favorite tunes, an audiobook, or a great podcast, fill your head with great stories, ideas, and fodder for inspiration as you drive.

Create Something

Use your phone's voice recorder—it's perfect for brainstorming or making lists. (Keep in mind that the translations aren't always perfect, so you might need to do some ducking editing after.)

Take a Different Route

You don't eat the same thing every single day, do you? So why take the same route to work every day? Once or twice a week, chose the route that's most pleasurable.

Treat Yourself

On the worst commute days, I plan to either stop along the way for a treat or have one waiting for me at the end of my drive.

Let Someone Else Drive

Consider carpooling with a work colleague or taking public transit. Both options are good for the environment, and allow you to catch up, read, write, or people watch.

Indulge Yourself

Go into a store and try on some clothes you can't afford.

THE BLISS OF WALKING

My love of walking was born from my relationship with my grandfather. Whenever he visited, he'd take a nightly walk. If we were lucky, he'd let one of us kids go with him. What was seductive about these walks was that I could ask him all the things I didn't yet feel comfortable asking other adults.

There's something profound about the conversations you can have with someone when you're walking beside them. Perhaps because you're not facing each other, you're more open to expressing hidden parts of yourself. Or it's simply that there's a rhythm that comes from walking that enables your souls to sync up.

On a recent hike, I noticed how quiet it was. All I could hear was the occasional rustling of leaves and softly singing bird. I breathed in the air deeply. I stood in awe of the ancient trees, covered in velvety moss, and I couldn't resist touching them. Their roots looked like long fingers wrapped around one another, as if they were holding each other like old lovers.

This may sound weird, but as I ventured deeper into the forest, it felt as though it came alive and was watching me with a kind, benevolent energy. The branches reached out and caressed me with their leaves, softly whispering to me. At one point I actually became weepy with the incredible beauty of it all. I stopped and sat for a long while, just being, and felt all my stresses fade away.

Lately, everywhere I look I find stories about the power of time spent in the woods. Being in open spaces with super-tall things makes you feel smaller, which helps you realize that your problems are small, too. The practice of *shinrin-yoku*— "forest bathing" or taking in your surroundings using your senses—has even spread all over the world. (Unlike traditional bathing, it's done fully clothed— although I suppose you could do it naked in remote areas if you wanted to.)

In our world of constant work and communication, there's something incredibly powerful about walking, and particularly walking in nature. So, if you're feeling stressed and disconnected, find a forest to explore, and let your heart lead you.

FIND YOUR PLEASURE

HUNT FOR TREASURES

There's something so timeless about treasure hunts.

When I was around sixteen, I decided to create a treasure hunt for my boyfriend's birthday. I carefully wrote down little riddles on paper and hid them around the city—one was placed in a favorite book that we had both read at the library, another was trapped under a rock at the spot we first kissed, and so on. The trail of clever crumbs I left for him eventually led to an abandoned barn where I was waiting, complete with a picnic I'd prepared.

You can re-create this kind of magic for anyone of any age. After noticing how captivated my son was with the idea of pirates and gold coins, we decided to create our very own adventure one weekend in my parents' backyard. We made clues out of pictures on colorful construction paper, put them in plastic sandwich bags, and buried them around my mother's garden. They all led to the final *X*-marked spot on a map that revealed a place under a tree where he uncovered a tiny gift. He was still talking about our scavenger hunt days later, which made me realize he got as much pleasure from the whole experience as I did.

There's even a whole community dedicated to the love of treasure hunting. In geocaching, players use GPS to find small objects hidden all over the world in various-size containers using clues (and at times, agility). Most times you leave the goodies behind, but if you do want to take something, the rule is you have to replace your find with an item of equal or better value.

It doesn't take much to plan a treasure hunt for a lover, friend, or child, and it's a great way to add even more tiny perks to the pleasures of wandering.

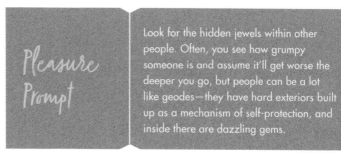

Pleasure Prompt

Look for the hidden jewels within other people. Often, you see how grumpy someone is and assume it'll get worse the deeper you go, but people can be a lot like geodes—they have hard exteriors built up as a mechanism of self-protection, and inside there are dazzling gems.

THE ALLURE OF NOSTALGIA

Ever wonder what it is about nostalgia that is so bewitching? The word *nostalgia* was apparently coined centuries ago by a Swiss physician to describe the sadness he witnessed in mercenaries who were aching to return home. Personally, I think of nostalgia as a strangely pleasurable feeling of wistfulness. One of the places I always get this feeling is at a fair. Let me explain.

Almost everyone has been to a fair. Perhaps you adore the bright lights, smell of popcorn or cotton candy, or thrilling sensation of being on the Ferris wheel. For me, it's the obnoxious rides, disgusting food, lazy farm animals, sweaty musicians, and beer. The barker shouting, "Step right up and behind this curtain you will see the most amazing sights. . . ." But then when you peek behind the curtain, it's not a new breed of lion but a grumpy cat with horns strapped on its head.

I love all of it. Everything is about selling the promise of something otherworldly, and utterly enchanting. I also love the undercurrent of sex and sin with a slight dash of terror. Not only because of my own memories, but also because I instantly feel transported back in time to the heyday of carnie culture. I wish I could go back to that time, to the crappy haunted houses with a date I could hang on to or whose arms I could jump into when I'm scared. Or go to the burlesque shows and watch the beautiful women in the sparkly gowns and intricate pasties. Instead of rude men shouting at them, there would be me, simply adoring them.

But I digress. See what happened there? I just got lost in nostalgia that doesn't even belong to me!

Numerous studies have shown that nostalgia can help affirm our sense of meaning in life and make us feel happier and more connected. One has even shown that when it's cold, people use nostalgia to warm themselves up.

I love that. The act of simply remembering something can actually change your body temperature. Magical.

Pleasure Project

Take the time to look through old family photos. If they only exist digitally, choose a few and print them out.

FIND YOUR PLEASURE

AN UNSCHEDULED DAY

Have you ever looked at your calendar and thought, *Dear Lord, how am I going to get through the next day/week/month?*

When that happens, you can use the wise advice of Sarah Knight, the fantastic author of the No F*cks Given guides, and break things down into small, manageable chunks so everything doesn't seem so overwhelming. But another thing you can do to prevent the feeling that you're drowning in insurmountable tasks is to schedule an unscheduled day.

The idea of an unscheduled day is to literally plan nothing and let the day unfold around you. It is actively saying, "Yes, I am aware that there are a whole bunch of things on my should-do and must-do lists. But, today, I am going to actively ignore all lists and only do what I feel like in the moment."

And when I say unscheduled, I mean unscheduled! So if you've planned a delightful brunch date with an old friend on your free day, it doesn't count. Because admit it: sometimes even getting together with friends you love can end up feeling like another item on your to-do list. But if you wake up and feel like going out for a coffee with a friend, then go right ahead. If you're inclined to bake a cake, you have my permission! Or if you decide to do nothing but rewatch bad rom-coms and wander aimlessly around—that's fine, too.

We often forget that it is in the quiet moments of our lives that some of the best ideas arise. When we indulge in silence and stillness, that's also when we can hear our inner voice begin to speak to us, the voice that can tell us secret truths that often get ignored in the hustle and bustle of everyday life.

So go ahead and cancel all your plans one day this month. Instead, let your spirit wander and find its pleasure.

FIND YOUR PLEASURE

PLAN A STAYCATION

If you're not a fan of winter, like me, but can't get away somewhere filled with luscious palm trees, hot-pink bougainvillea, and coconut-scented everything yet desperately need a vacation, here are tips on how to make a staycation feel infused with the impressions that go along with an escape.

- Pools at the local community center are fantastic. But for a step up from that, many hotels issue day passes for their water facilities. Or book yourself into a spa with a hot tub and treat yourself to a massage!

- Stay at an Airbnb, a "no tell" hotel, or a fancy place. To save money, ask someone to take your kid(s) for a night and sleep in another room in your own home.

- Get cozy by a fireplace. Close your eyes, soak up the heat, and you might almost convince yourself the sun is beating down on you!

- We all need time away from the constant barrage of depressing news and pressure to be perfect. So turn off your technology.

- For a fabulous sun-kissed glow, get a spray tan. It can even out and brighten your skin, making it look like you've just returned from a luxurious trip.

- If you're feeling stir-crazy, hop in the car and visit a neighborhood you've never been before—the coffee shops and bakeries, restaurants, stores, and galleries. Or check out a map, and explore a small town nearby.

Kindness

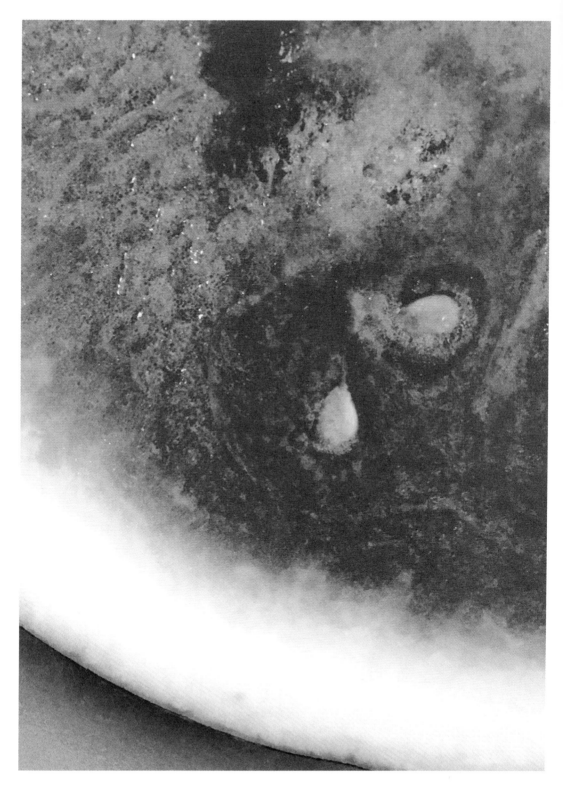

FIND YOUR PLEASURE

RANDOM ACTS OF KINDNESS

E very day we have the opportunity to choose kindness, to plant little seeds of pleasure everywhere we go. Here are some ideas.

Be Kind to Yourself

Have you ever felt guilty about how you spend your time or money? Relived a mistake you made? The next time that inner voice reminds you of your flaws, replace it with words of kindness. Maybe you haven't been exercising enough, but you're spending more time with family and friends. Maybe you're a working mother worried that you're missing out on milestones, but you're showing your child how important meaningful work is. Maybe you said something you regret, but mistakes are how you learn and grow. Remember, kindness starts with you.

Listen to Others

Tune into the emotional temperature of the people you encounter: the barista at your favorite coffee shop, the front desk person at your gym, the checkout clerk at the grocery store. Ask how they are and actually listen to the answer (not just what they say but also *how* they say it).

Send Notes

It only takes a few minutes to send an email of appreciation or write a handwritten note, and there's nothing like the pleasure of receiving a message from a friend.

Just Do It

All around us, every day, there are people who are lonely, who are struggling, who don't want to be an imposition. So when you see someone in need, rather than asking if there is anything you can do, just *do* something to help.

Celebrate Kindness

Seek out and share stories of people doing incredible things. The more we hold up the everyday heroes in our midst, the more others will be inspired to make room for kindness in their own lives.

FIND YOUR PLEASURE

A SPOONFUL OF SWEETNESS

I'm sure we all think of ourselves as pretty nice people generally. But admit it: when you're stressed, scared, or exhausted, that can change.

There's a parking lot near my work owned by a curmudgeonly dude. I was paying one day, and he tried to charge me more than usual. When I pointed that out, he shouted, "I'll charge whatever I want." A huge part of me wanted to say, "Go fuck yourself!" But I need to park there. So I bit my tongue and left.

The next day he looked me right in the eyes. He told me I was in after 9:00 a.m., so there was going to be an extra charge again. *I seethed.* The third day I was running late and was driving with hatred coursing through my veins. I fantasized about how I would yell at him, threaten to blast him on social media. Then it dawned on me: if I said anything with anger, nothing would change—except I'd have to find a new place to park. So I decided to change my approach.

As I walked up to him, I pictured him as an overgrown, wounded boy with a mean father who taught him to be a jerk. I have zero idea if the story I concocted was remotely true, but it allowed me to see him as a whole person. I also realized I could come off as patronizing if I didn't hit exactly the right tone. But someone had to raise the white flag. I said sweetly, "Good morning," and handed him my money with a sincere smile. He looked at me with utter confusion, charged me the cheaper amount, and let me go. Since then, he has been nothing but pleasant.

Besides making that awful situation better, I've recently discovered there are many reasons to be sweeter. A study has found that pleasure often comes from being nice to others. It makes us happy, improves our outlook, and gives us a sense of well-being. Kind people see the world as a better place. Other studies have found that those who took part in a compassion meditation course had significantly lower levels of cortisol (a stress hormone that can lead to heart disease, cancer, and depression) than those who didn't, and that people who help others are more desirable, have more sexual partners, and more frequent sex.

So the next time you feel your rage rising, take a deep breath—after all, if you treat others well, you'll end up feeling good, too!

Pleasure Project

Have a "no complaining" day. See if you can stretch it into a week. A year?

GLEEFUL GOSSIP

When I was in university, a friend and I started this game that we called "Tell Last." Whenever we were together, the last thing we'd do before going our separate ways was pass on good gossip we'd heard about each other. So she'd say something like, "I heard Diane say that she thinks you have an exquisite side profile." And I'd say, "Joel told me he thinks you are the reincarnation of Anaïs Nin."

Ridiculous stuff, right? But the impact was *delicious*!

Think about how many times in a day you hear nice things about someone. Unfortunately, that stuff mostly never crosses their ears. (Except maybe at their funeral. How tragic is it that people often wait until someone has died before talking about all of the wonderful ways in which they've touched other people?) Yet nasty gossip seems to constantly flow. So why not intentionally counter some of that? Who knows, maybe you'll start a new trend that focuses on enhancing all that is so great about people—and particularly women.

Pleasure Prompt

Go out of your way to "like" other women's photos on social media. Or better yet, amplify the voices of women whose stories often don't get told. Feel the pleasure of supporting other women.

THE VULNERABILITY OF KINDNESS

Kindness, at its heart, is an exercise in vulnerability and empathy. It's interesting that we often say "practice" kindness, as if we intuitively understand that it is work, that it can be challenging, and that sometimes we must remind ourselves how to do it.

You need only peek into social media to witness how the worst aspects of people have been able to flourish. Hidden behind kitten and egg avatars, many people get a real charge from being awful. Assuming the worst of others and delighting in public failures is cynicism wrapped in jealousy sprinkled with a bit of anger. People eat up that sort of thing with reckless (and feckless) abandon.

And can we be honest here? There *can* be a kind of easy, decadent pleasure that comes from watching the worst of the mighty fail. To see them fall on their own self-righteous swords. It isn't kind, but I think we can all acknowledge that it is human. The problem is that this kind of pleasure confection is short-term, arguably addictive, and not great for our souls.

Choosing kindness is more challenging but infinitely more pleasurable. And we should never mistake kindness for weakness. It requires strength to see people, warts and all, yet still view them nonjudgmentally and compassionately. When you are able to do this, any risks you take getting to know people and seeking intimacy can become one of the greatest sources of happiness in life and provide huge rewards.

So let's not give up on kindness.

Pleasure Project

Email ten of your closest friends or family members. Ask them to send you a list of five words they'd use to describe you. Make a list of the words that come up most and put them in your pleasure pouch (see The Pleasure Within on page 163 to find out how to make one).

FIND YOUR PLEASURE

THINK GRATITUDE

I know: You hear the word *gratitude* and you roll your eyes. Me, too, sometimes. Often, it's just easier to complain.

Here's me at the grocery-store checkout with my inner voice screaming: *Why don't they have more cashiers? Why is this person buying so much stuff? Can't this move any faster?!* All the while, I'm not only not changing anything, but I'm also making myself more miserable.

And once when I was jogging, my inner voice was saying, *Ugh. I hate this. Why do I do this? I can't wait to get home.* I wasn't enjoying any of it. As I slowed to a walk to catch my breath, an old man who was watering his garden nearby said to me, "Wow, I would do anything to run like that."

Point made, universe.

Part of angst like that comes from rushing around, having too many to-do lists and being time crunched. So the next time you're caught in a traffic jam, line, or other time-sucking/frustrating situation, try some of these ideas:

Breathe deeply—just a few deep breaths can instantly lower tension.

Think like a kid: look around you, find patterns in colors or numbers,
people watch, bounce a bit, sing a song.

Consider all the things that have made you happy today. Go
into the minutiae! You are alive!

Pick something pleasurable that you'll do—buy yourself an ice-cream cone,
have a nice bath, touch yourself—
as soon as you're out of your unpleasurable pickle.

Pleasure Project

Start a best part–worst part practice in your home. Take turns talking about
what the best parts of your day are and share the worst parts. Then talk
about what you could do to make the worst parts better if they ever happen again.
This beautiful ritual will not only help connect you with each other but also
remind you that tomorrow is another day to make both mistakes and magic.

VOLUNTEER TIME

Anyone who has ever been sick, given birth, or gone through another major life change knows that it's those little gestures from others that really make a difference. The person who brings the lasagna and leaves it at your door. The individual who comes by to put a smile on your face. The friend who sits with you and just listens.

No matter how much or how little you have, no matter what kind of money you make, you can always give your time.

When we hear the word *volunteer*, what often comes to mind is working at a soup kitchen or picking up garbage from a nearby park. Those things are immensely valuable. But if you haven't felt moved to volunteer because they're the only things you think of, keep in mind that there are plenty of other options that will suit your particular passions and skill set.

For instance, if you're passionate about politics, join a political campaign. If you're a craft queen, knit or sew a blanket for someone in need. If you love babies, find a hospital program that allows you to cuddle newborns. Adore dogs? Join a city program to walk them. Have a passion for travel? Join an outreach group and help build not only homes but also connections all over the world.

The pleasures of volunteering are endless. People who volunteer are happier and healthier than those who don't. Older people who volunteer tend to live longer. Through volunteering, you'll hear people's stories, expand your view of the world, and no longer be thinking about your own problems but will be focused on helping someone else.

What could be more pleasurable than that?

FIND YOUR PLEASURE

EMBRACE EMPATHY

I once heard a story about a father who was on the subway. His kids were running around and disturbing all the passengers while the father sat there doing nothing. Eventually one person got up and said to him, "Excuse me, but can you do something about your kids?" The father said, "Oh, yes, sorry," in a bit of a daze. "They just found out their mother died, so I guess we're all in a bit of a state . . ."

How often do we see a person doing something we don't like or approve of—whether it's a shitty driver or a social media bragger—and automatically think the worst of them? It's so much easier for us to see them as the enemy than to perhaps consider what might be going on in their world.

What if, instead, when you find yourself in those situations, you reached for empathy rather than ire? The great thing about doing that is as soon as you release your frustrations and anger, you go from being tight and tense to loose and relaxed. So the next time you feel your blood begin to boil, try actively choosing calm instead.

Pleasure Project

Think about what you want people to say about you after you are dead. Decide how you will become that person.

PLEASURES OF

the colour ye
lamps, fans
stuffed toys
injera bread
peace times
_____

sunlight
sleep
freedom
autonomy

eig
rea
gree
easy
lin
sleep

De

m

sn

FIND YOUR PLEASURE

Sometimes the world can feel like a hostile place—especially online. But there is beauty that can calm you if you look for it. And if you're having a hard time finding it, why not create it yourself?

I was once caught in my daily commute of traffic jams and happened to notice signs on the side of a building that read "Pleasures of Living"—I kid you not. But every time I tried to get a closer look, the traffic would start moving again. So one day I decided to make a special trip to find those signs and take a closer look. It turned out that they were hand-painted, and by then they'd been eroded somewhat by the weather, but I could still make them out.

Whoever created them had very specific pleasures of living, and they included: the color yellow, lamps and fans, stuffed toys, diversity, neighborhoods, lingerie, and smells.

The instructions in their recipe for cultivating more pleasure involved the following: buy ultra-happy eggs; find a pie-making, country-music-loving, boyfriend; think positively about mankind; shower more; and take it easy.

The signs were both a public declaration and a call to action.

They got me thinking that I should make my own list of my pleasures of living. So I unearthed some of my son's construction paper and wrote out the following using bright, colorful markers:

Lazy, unscheduled days

Vacation sex

The smell of my lover's neck

The sound of my son's laugh

Sexy sushi rolls served with edible flowers

The first sip of a brilliant Shiraz

Good debates

Bad horror movies

Warm, fresh sheets

Cool water on a hot day

Waking up in a hotel room in a different part of the world

Random acts of kindness

Then I took that paper and I put it in a bottle and sent it off to sea. My hope was that someone halfway across the world would find it, so I could share it, and they would be inspired to create their own list, just as I was.

I'm hoping that this will inspire you to do the same. Write your secret pleasures with abandon on a piece of paper. Now go and give it away.

FOCUS ON GOOD THINGS

It's said that writing down three to five things that you're grateful for every day gives you a 25 percent happiness boost. I'm not sure how reliable that statistic is, but try it anyway—what do you have to lose?

It's easy, too! Start by tapping into your senses. What can you see around you that brings pleasure: Is there a photo of someone you love? An item that brings you fond memories? What can you feel? Is there a comfortable blanket you're sitting on? Is there something you can grab to make you cozier? Is there something you hear that's calming? A bird in the distance? A song you love? What can you taste? Are you sipping a fruity tea? Nibbling on something sweet or savory?

This activity has the added benefit of calming our minds, while also turning our attention to or allowing us to zoom into the small things in our lives that bring joy. Even if you don't write these things down, try saying out loud what you see, hear, or feel and are thankful for.

There is also something called "beginner's mind" that is often used to help calm those with anxiety or depression. The idea is to approach everything—including ourselves—with a sense of curiosity and awe instead of judgment or shame. This simple act helps ground us in the present, prevents us from spiraling into an abyss of gloom, and allows us to tap into the tiniest of pleasures that are always around us.

These activities will not only make you feel great, they'll make you more disposed to act kindly toward others, and what wonderful joy there is in that!

FIND YOUR PLEASURE

PAY IT FORWARD

One day, I was at the grocery store just after the holidays and there was a man in front of me at the checkout. He was told that his bank card was declined and he ran out, while I just stood there like an idiot, my face in my phone.

For a long time afterward, I deeply regretted that I didn't chase him down and pay for his groceries. It would have been a simple thing that could have radically changed that man's day.

I was reminded of that recently when I saw a viral video of two men who stepped in to pay for a woman's gas. They noticed that she was paying with pennies, and recognized that she needed help, so they reached out to her only to find out that she had recently lost her husband. Moved by their sudden and unexpected act of kindness, she began crying, and then the men started crying, and then I started crying witnessing the beautiful humanity of it all.

It was one of the most touching things I have seen in a long time—and a potent reminder of how little it takes to pay pleasure forward.

Pleasure Prompt

For one month, only share inspirational stories or features about warriors for positive change on your social media feeds. See how you feel by the end.

FIND YOUR PLEASURE

SHARE SOMETHING YOU LOVE

I love macarons. I'm not talking about macaroons—those little chocolate confections made with coconut (although they are also delicious). Macarons are those delicate soft, chewy, pastel-colored French pastries that come in a whole variety of flavors, from chocolate to raspberry to pistachio and salted caramel.

I'm aware that they are a divisive confection, so I'm fully willing to acknowledge that you may not find the pleasure in them that I do. But if you haven't tried one yet, I'd like you to know that I would derive great pleasure if you decided upon my recommendation to sample some—and ended up *loving* them.

There is something so pleasurable about not only sharing something you love with someone else, but also having them fall just as deeply and passionately in love with it, isn't there? Whether it's a piece of music, a work of art, a favorite book, a secret location, or a delicious treat, introducing something that holds deep and rich meaning to another person is like creating a kind of sweet game of pleasure tag. So go out and hit someone up with your favorite thing and then ask them to pass it on.

You're it!

Indulge Yourself

Call someone you love just so you can hear his or her voice.

FIND YOUR PLEASURE

AFTERWORD

I discovered while working on this book that the process of writing is a little like going on a treasure hunt within yourself—or should I say pleasure hunt? You're constantly turning over stones of your life to see what enchantments lie within, mining your mind for little nuggets of truth, poetry, and insight in the hopes that your stories will resonate with other people. And once you uncover something golden, you realize how vital it is to capture these moments, these stories, to create maps of sorts so that you can always find your way back to them again.

With that in mind, I'd like to suggest that you start to develop your own maps—what I call pleasure maps. Like treasure maps, these will direct you and others to the hidden jewels inside of you. You can create a pleasure map for your life, your day, or your body. Here's how:

Think deeply about the things buried deep within you—the ideas that wake you sometimes in the middle of the night, demanding attention, those tiny things that poke away at you. Perhaps it's a yearning for a new job or relationship, a passion for better sex, a desire for more authenticity. Pick one and write it down. Mark it with an X.

Draw the path you will need to take to get where you want to go. If it's a new job, or a new relationship, what steps will you need to take in order to reach that destination? If it's better sex, what are the areas of your body that you need explored and how should they be touched? Will the terrain in certain areas be difficult to get through? Why? How will you make your way?

Make a plan. What tools or supplies will you need to unearth those pleasures? If you want a new job, maybe you need to take some classes. If you're searching for time to write, maybe you need more help around the house. If your goal is more orgasms, maybe you need some gadgets or to give your partner your pleasure map.

Begin your journey. Every day, take another little step further. And don't forget to reward yourself at the end of your journey.

Remember, there's gold in those hills. Now go and find it!

CYNTHIA'S PRINCIPLES OF PLEASURE

Life is meant to be profoundly enjoyed.

The path to true pleasure is through getting to know yourself.

The only way you will get to know yourself is by slowing down.

Listen to that inner voice.

Make time for play.

You are your own best lover.

Sometimes, less is more.

Perfection is boring.

If you feel guilty about your pleasures, you're not doing them right.

Life is too short for constant self-deprivation.

Feel it all.

Pleasure Project

What are your pleasure principles?
Write them down.

My Pleasure Principles

MY PLEASURE PRINCIPLES

Acknowledgments

Huge thanks and love to my agent, Danny Fritz, and the entire team at SBX, especially McKenzie Clarke. I'm so delighted to be on this journey with you by my side.

To Nita Pronovost and the team at Simon & Schuster—thank you for getting behind this idea right from the get-go.

Endless love to my editors Laurie Grassi and Sarah St. Pierre at Simon & Schuster. Thanks for understanding my voice, making my words better, and being endlessly enthusiastic about this project. You were truly such a pleasure to work with.

My parents, Diane and Dale, my sister, Kari, and my entire extended family for believing in me and instilling in me the essentials for a pleasure-filled life (basically chips, wine, games, and walks).

To Chin and Andie. Thank you for loving Jaya and helping me on a daily basis. You are my village.

To the team at CTV Bellmedia, especially Nanci MacLean for being a wonderful leader and a treasured friend. Also Michelle Crespi, Laura Scarfo, and the entire *The Social* production team, along with our incredible crew and glam squad, for making work a pleasure every day. And of course my *The Social* sisters: Melissa Grelo, Lainey Lui, Marci Ien, and Jessica Allen for always having my back.

To Jann Arden, Diane Borsato, Jenny Prior, Jaelyn Galbraith, Teddy Wilson, Cory Silverberg, Hester Koopman, Sunday Muse, Sam Maggs, Traci Melchor, Tyrone Edwards, and Roula Said—thank you for listening to me, reading parts of this and/or letting me share your stories, and just being all-around wonderful people. I love you.

Shayna Haddon—for all of your foresight and insight in helping to create this project.

Mad love to Diane Borsato, Alkan Emin, Keri Knapp, Thomas Smythe, Max Wells, Janet Zablocki, Melissa Grelo, and Kari Loyst for contributing some beautiful photographs, as well as Whitespace Creative for creative consulting. Also to Chinkok Tan, Agnes Ivan, and Jennifer Murphy for allowing me to feature your art in the background of a few of these photos. To Alex and Sandra Lianos from The Hartman for allowing us to shoot a few photos in your beautiful space, and thanks to Alex Marconi from St. Regis Toronto.

For being sources of inspiration in so many different ways: Iris Apfel; Sara Benincasa; Paul Bloom; Shannon Boodram; Nova Browning Rutherford; Julia

Cameron; Cat and Nat; Gary Chapman; Rose Cousins; Lena Dunham; Sallie Foley and my entire cohort in the University of Michigan's Sexual Health program; Nancy Friday; Ina May Gaskin; Elizabeth Gilbert; John Gottman; Lauren Holly; Arianna Huffington; Corita Kent; Farrah Khan; Sarah Knight; Beyoncé Knowles-Carter; Melissa Leong; Jason Logan; Selena Luna; Erica Lust; Rachel Mielke; Thomas Moore; Emily Nagoski, PhD; Tuppy Owens; Esther Perel; Shonda Rhimes; Sark; Vivek Shraya; Emilia Symyington Fedy; and Dr. Sheila Wijayasinghe.

All of the contributors on findyourpleasure.com—especially Aggie Armstrong, Jeni Besworth, Kelly Boutsalis, Dr. Allie Carter, Beverley Kesse, Michelle Melles, Andrea Slaney, and Sarah Sahagian—your words have brought so much joy into the world. Thanks for being fellow pleasure pushers. I adore you all.

Readers of findyourpleasure.com—thank you for your thoughtful comments and unwavering support. We do this for you.

For anyone else who may recognize themselves in these stories—thank you for teaching me about life, love and pleasure.

Photography Credits

Savoring Moments, The Pleasure of Touch, Make a Date, and A Spoonful of Sweetness: Keri Knapp.

Al Fresco Fun: Max Wells.

Quality Time: Melissa Grelo.

The Language of Food: Diane Borsato; background art by Jennifer Murphy.

Wonder Walls: background art by Chinkok Tan.

The Wonder of Pregnancy, Milestones, Change Your Position, In Praise of Slow, and Random Acts of Kindness: Kari Loyst.

The Joys of Nursing: Janet Zablocki.

The Key to "Casual" Sex, Learn to Plork, An Unscheduled Day, and Volunteer Time: Thomas Smythe.

Pleasurable Workdays: background art by Agnes Ivan.

Prepare and Practice: Blair Deveny.

Afterword: Alkan Emin.

All other photographs: Jason and Cynthia Loyst.

About the Author

CYNTHIA LOYST is co-host of CTV's *The Social*, a writer, producer, television host, and self-described "professional sensualist." She is also the creator of findyourpleasure, a popular online destination that celebrates decadence, indulgence, and pure, unadulterated joy. She is also a sought-after public speaker and relationship-advice columnist. *Find Your Pleasure* is her debut book. Visit her at **findyourpleasure.com** or follow her on Twitter or Instagram at **@fypleasure** and **@cynthialoyst**.